THE AUSTRALIAN
Women's Weekly
simple roasts

THE AUSTRALIAN
Women's Weekly

contents

The word roast brings to mind images of Sundays, family, and flavoursome comfort food. The roast is a sure-fire crowd-pleaser, and by putting the tips and recipes in this book into action you'll have perfect results every time. With family and friends around, and a delicious, warm roast on the table, things couldn't be better. Enjoy…

Food Director

Pamela Clark

classic roast chicken

1.8kg whole chicken
2 tablespoons olive oil
6 medium potatoes (1kg), halved
2 tablespoons plain flour
2 cups (500ml) chicken stock
1 cup (250ml) water

bacon & leek stuffing
40g butter
2 rashers rindless bacon (130g),
chopped finely
1 small leek (200g), sliced thinly
2 trimmed celery stalks (200g),
chopped finely
2 cups (140g) stale breadcrumbs
1 egg, beaten lightly
1 tablespoon coarsely chopped
fresh sage

1 Preheat oven to 200°C/180°C fan-assisted. Make stuffing.
2 Wash chicken under cold running water; pat dry inside and out with absorbent paper. Tuck wing tips under chicken. Trim skin around neck; secure to underside of chicken with toothpicks.
3 Fill cavity with bacon & leek stuffing; tie legs together with string. Place chicken on oiled wire rack in large flameproof baking dish. Rub chicken all over with half the oil; roast, uncovered, 1½ hours.
4 Meanwhile, boil, steam or microwave potato 5 minutes; drain. Combine potato and remaining oil in large shallow baking dish; roast, uncovered, alongside chicken 1 hour, turning occasionally during roasting. Remove chicken from oven; cover to keep warm. Remove and discard toothpicks.
5 Increase oven temperature to 240°C/220°C fan-assisted. Roast potato, uncovered, further 15 minutes or until browned and crisp.

6 Meanwhile, drain all but 2 tablespoons of the juices from chicken dish, add flour; cook, stirring over medium heat, until mixture thickens and bubbles. Gradually add combined stock and the water, stirring until gravy boils and thickens. Strain into large jug. Serve with chicken and potatoes.

bacon & leek stuffing
Melt butter in medium frying pan; cook bacon, leek and celery until vegetables are tender, cool. Combine bacon mixture in medium bowl with breadcrumbs, egg and sage.

preparation time 20 minutes
cooking time 1 hour 30 minutes
(plus cooling time)
serves 4
nutritional count per serving 61.3g total fat (20.5g saturated fat); 4320kJ (1046 cal); 56.0g carbohydrate; 65.3g protein; 6.5g fibre

chicken & poultry

lemon thyme roast chicken

1.8kg whole chicken
40g butter
1 large onion (200g), chopped finely
2 cloves garlic, crushed
4 rashers rindless bacon (260g), chopped finely
1 egg, beaten lightly
1½ cups (105g) stale breadcrumbs
1 tablespoon chopped fresh lemon thyme
80g butter, extra, softened
¼ teaspoon sea salt flakes
12 small carrots (840g)

1 Preheat oven to 200°C/180°C fan-assisted. Oil large flameproof roasting dish.

2 Wash chicken and pat dry with absorbent paper.

3 Heat butter in medium frying pan; cook onion, garlic and bacon, stirring, until onion is soft. Remove from heat; cool 5 minutes.

4 Combine bacon mixture, egg, breadcrumbs and 2 teaspoons of thyme in medium bowl. Fill cavity of chicken with seasoning.

5 Combine extra butter and 1 teaspoon of the remaining thyme in small bowl. Carefully separate the skin from the breast of chicken with your fingers; spread herb butter under skin covering breast. Secure skin over cavity with toothpicks. Tie legs together with kitchen string; tuck wings underneath. Rub remaining thyme and salt over skin.

6 Place chicken in baking dish; roast, uncovered, for 20 minutes. Add carrots; roast further 40 minutes or until chicken is cooked through. Stand, covered, for 10 minutes. Remove and discard tothpicks.

7 Sprinkle chicken with extra thyme leaves and salt, if desired. Serve with carrots.

preparation time 20 minutes
cooking time 1 hour 10 minutes (plus cooling and standing times)
serves 4
nutritional count per serving 71.9g total fat (31.3g saturated fat); 4335kJ (1037 cal); 30.3g carbohydrate; 65.1g protein; 7.3g fibre

2 bulbs garlic
2kg whole chicken
cooking-oil spray
2 teaspoons salt
2 tablespoons cracked black
pepper
1 medium lemon (140g), cut into
eight wedges
1 cup (250ml) water
3 medium globe artichokes
(660g)
2 tablespoons lemon juice
2 medium red onions (340g),
quartered
3 baby fennel bulbs (390g),
trimmed, halved
2 medium leeks (700g), halved
lengthways then quartered
250g cherry tomatoes
1/3 cup (80ml) dry white wine
1/4 cup (60ml) lemon juice, extra

1 Preheat oven to 200°C/180°C
fan-assisted.
2 Separate cloves from garlic
bulb, leaving skin intact. Wash
chicken under cold water; pat dry
inside and out with absorbent
paper. Coat chicken with cooking-
oil spray; press combined salt and
pepper onto skin and inside cavity.
Place garlic and lemon inside
cavity; tie legs together with
kitchen string. Place chicken on
small oiled wire rack in large
flameproof baking dish, pour the
water in baking dish; roast,
uncovered, 50 minutes.
3 Meanwhile, discard outer leaves
from artichokes; cut tips from
remaining leaves. Trim then peel
stalks. Quarter artichokes
lengthways; using teaspoon
remove chokes. Cover artichoke
with cold water in medium bowl,
stir in the 2 tablespoons of lemon
juice; soak until required.

4 Add drained artichoke, onion,
fennel and leek to dish; coat with
cooking-oil spray. Roast,
uncovered, 40 minutes or until
vegetables are just tender.
5 Add tomatoes to dish; roast,
uncovered, about 20 minutes or
until tomatoes soften and chicken
is cooked through. Place chicken
on serving dish and vegetables in
large bowl; cover to keep warm.
6 Stir wine and extra juice into
dish with pan juices; bring to the
boil. Boil 2 minutes then strain

sauce over vegetables; toss gently
to combine.
7 Discard garlic and lemon from
cavity; serve chicken with
vegetables.

preparation time 35 minutes
cooking time 1 hour 50 minutes
serves 4
nutritional count per serving
35.7g total fat (10.7g saturated
fat); 2859kJ (684 cal); 18.8g
carbohydrate; 62.0g protein;
14.6g fibre

pepper-roasted garlic
& lemon chicken

Sometimes known as piri-piri chicken after Portugal's favourite spicy hot sauce, this style of cooking chicken has become a runaway success, winning customers from traditional deep-fried, spit-roast or barbecued chicken shops.

tips add one or two more chillies to the spice mixture for a hotter flavour. If desired, marinate chicken in chilli mixture, covered, in the refrigerator, overnight; turning constantly to coat each side. You can use chicken pieces rather than a whole chicken if you prefer: try a mixture of whole thighs and drumsticks, marylands or whole breasts… just remember to reduce the cooking time.

1.6kg whole chicken
1 fresh small red thai chilli, deseeded, chopped finely
1 tablespoon sweet paprika
3 cloves garlic, crushed
2 teaspoons salt
½ cup (125ml) lemon juice
2 tablespoons olive oil
1 tablespoon coarsely chopped fresh oregano

1 Preheat oven to 160°C/140°C fan-assisted.

2 Wash chicken under cold running water; pat dry with absorbent paper. Using kitchen scissors, cut along both sides of backbone; discard backbone. Place chicken, skin-side up, on board; using heel of hand, press down on breastbone to flatten chicken. Insert metal skewer through thigh and opposite wing of chicken to keep chicken flat. Repeat with other thigh and wing.

3 Combine remaining ingredients in small bowl.

4 Place chicken in large baking dish; pour over chilli mixture. Roast, uncovered, brushing occasionally with pan juices, about 2 hours or until chicken is browned and cooked through. Remove skewers. Serve with roasted vegetables.

preparation time 15 minutes
cooking time 2 hours
serves 4
nutritional count per serving 41.4g total fat (11.3g saturated fat); 2232kJ (534 cal); 1.1g carbohydrate; 40.3g protein; 0.4g fibre

slow-roasted portuguese chicken

roast chicken with red onions, garlic & cherries

1.8kg whole chicken
3 sprigs fresh thyme
½ lemon
10 cloves garlic
30g butter, softened
3 medium red onions (500g),
cut into wedges
2 tablespoons olive oil
1½ cups (225g) fresh cherries

1 Preheat oven to 180°C/160°C fan-assisted.
2 Wash the cavity of the chicken under cold water; pat dry with absorbent paper. Insert two of the thyme sprigs, lemon and two of the garlic cloves into the cavity. Tuck wings under chicken, tie chicken legs together with kitchen string.
3 Place chicken, breast-side up, on oiled wire rack in small roasting dish. Rub chicken all over with softened butter; roast, uncovered, 20 minutes.
4 Combine onion, remaining garlic and oil in medium baking dish. Roast onion mixture alongside chicken further 50 minutes.
5 Add cherries to onion mixture, toss gently to combine; sprinkle remaining thyme over chicken. Roast chicken and cherry mixture further 10 minutes or until chicken is tender and cherries are hot.

preparation time 20 minutes
cooking time 1 hour 20 minutes
serves 4
nutritional count per serving 51.8g total fat (16.7g saturated fat); 2955kJ (707 cal); 11.8g carbohydrate; 47.6g protein; 3.8g fibre

southern fried chicken with buttermilk mash and gravy

20 chicken drumsticks (1.4kg)
1 cup (250ml) buttermilk
1 cup (150g) plain flour
¼ cup cajun seasoning
½ cup (125ml) vegetable oil
40g butter
5 medium potatoes (1kg), chopped coarsely
¾ cup (180ml) buttermilk, warmed, extra
40g butter, extra
250g green beans, trimmed, cut into 4cm lengths
2 cups (500ml) chicken stock

1 Combine chicken and buttermilk in large bowl. Cover; refrigerate 3 hours or overnight. Drain; discard buttermilk.
2 Combine flour and seasoning in large bowl; add chicken, toss to coat in mixture. Cover; refrigerate about 30 minutes or until flour forms a paste.
3 Preheat oven to 240°C/220°C fan-assisted.
4 Heat oil and butter in large deep frying pan; shake excess paste from chicken back into bowl. Cook chicken, in batches, over medium heat until browned and crisp.
5 Place chicken on oiled wire rack over large baking dish; roast, covered, in oven 15 minutes. Uncover; roast about 10 minutes or until chicken is cooked through and crisp.
6 Meanwhile, boil, steam or microwave potato until tender; drain. Mash with extra buttermilk and extra butter until smooth. Cover to keep warm.
7 Boil, steam or microwave beans until tender; drain.
8 To make gravy, add excess paste to pan; cook, stirring, until mixture bubbles. Gradually stir in stock; cook, stirring, until gravy boils and thickens. Strain gravy into large jug.
9 Serve chicken with mash, beans and gravy.

preparation time 20 minutes (plus refrigeration time)
cooking time 40 minutes
serves 4
nutritional count per serving 69.7g total fat (22.6g saturated fat); 4585kJ (1097 cal); 64.3g carbohydrate; 50.4g protein; 6.6g fibre

tip cajun seasoning is available from the spice section at the supermarket.

10 large chicken wings (1.2kg)
2 tablespoons honey
2 tablespoons soy sauce
2 fresh small red thai chillies, chopped finely

fried rice

1 tablespoon groundnut oil
2 eggs, beaten lightly
4 rashers rindless bacon (260g), chopped coarsely
3 spring onions, sliced thinly
½ cup (60g) frozen peas
½ cup (80g) frozen corn kernels
1 tablespoon soy sauce
3 cups cold cooked white long-grain rice

1 Preheat oven to 200°C/180°C fan-assisted.
2 Cut wings into three pieces at joints; discard wing tips. Combine wings, honey, sauce and chilli in large bowl.
3 Place undrained wings, in single layer, on oiled wire rack in large shallow baking dish; reserve any marinade in bowl. Roast, uncovered, brushing wings with marinade occasionally, about 40 minutes or until browned and cooked through, turning halfway through cooking time.
4 Meanwhile, make fried rice.
5 Serve wings accompanied with fried rice.

fried rice heat half of the oil in wok; cook egg over medium heat, swirling wok to form thin omelette. Remove from pan; cool. Roll omelette, cut into thin slices. Heat remaining oil in same wok; stir-fry bacon until crisp. Add remaining ingredients and omelette slices; stir-fry until hot.

tip You need to cook 1½ cups (300g) white long-grain rice the day before making this recipe. Spread cooled cooked rice on a tray, cover; refrigerate overnight.

preparation time 15 minutes
cooking time 40 minutes (plus cooling time)
serves 4
nutritional count per serving 23.1g total fat (6.9g saturated fat); 2876kJ (688 cal); 57.2g carbohydrate; 61.3g protein; 2.8g fibre

chinese barbecue wings with fried rice

caramelised chicken thighs

2 teaspoons vegetable oil
4 chicken thigh cutlets (800g), skin on
1 medium red onion (170g), sliced thinly
3 cloves garlic, sliced thinly
¼ cup (55g) brown sugar
1 tablespoon dark soy sauce
1 tablespoon fish sauce
⅓ cup coarsely chopped fresh coriander

1 Preheat oven to 200°C/180°C fan-assisted.
2 Heat oil in large frying pan; cook chicken, both sides, until browned. Place chicken, in single layer, in baking dish. Roast, uncovered, in oven, about 25 minutes or until cooked through.
3 Meanwhile, heat same frying pan; cook onion and garlic, stirring, until onion softens. Add sugar and sauces; cook, stirring, 3 minutes.
4 Return chicken to pan with coriander; turn chicken to coat in mixture.

preparation time 20 minutes
cooking time 35 minutes
serves 4
nutritional count per serving 22.4g total fat (6.9g saturated fat); 1538kJ (368 cal); 16.3g carbohydrate; 24.8g protein; 1.0g fibre

tandoori chicken wings

16 small chicken wings (1.3kg)
½ cup (150g) tandoori paste
½ cup (140g) natural yogurt
1 medium onion (150g), grated

1 Preheat oven to 220°C/200°C fan-assisted.
2 Cut wings into three pieces at joints; discard tips. Combine chicken and remaining ingredients in large bowl. Cover; refrigerate 3 hours or overnight.
3 Place chicken, in single layer, on oiled wire rack set inside large shallow baking dish. Roast, uncovered, about 30 minutes or until chicken is well browned and cooked through.
4 Serve wings with lime wedges, if desired.

preparation time 10 minutes (plus refrigeration time)
cooking time 30 minutes
makes 32
nutritional count per wing 3.0g total fat (0.7g saturated fat); 234kJ (56 cal); 0.8g carbohydrate; 6.4g protein; 0.5g fibre

baba ghanoush pierce aubergines all over with fork; place on oiled oven tray. Roast, uncovered, about 40 minutes or until aubergines are soft, turning occasionally. Stand 10 minutes. Peel aubergines, discard skin; drain aubergines in colander 10 minutes. Blend or process aubergines with garlic, tahini, juice and oil.

8 chicken drumsticks (1.2kg)
2 teaspoons ground allspice
1 teaspoon ground black pepper
1 teaspoon ground cumin
2 tablespoons olive oil
4 large pittas

baba ghanoush
2 medium aubergines (600g)
1 clove garlic, crushed
1 tablespoon tahini
¼ cup (60ml) lemon juice
2 tablespoons olive oil

1 Preheat oven to 200°C/180°C fan-assisted.
2 Make baba ghanoush.
3 Meanwhile, combine drumsticks, spices and oil in large bowl.
4 Place drumsticks on oiled wire rack over baking dish. Roast, uncovered, about 50 minutes or until chicken is cooked through, turning occasionally.
5 Serve drumsticks with baba ghanoush and pitta and, if desired, lemon wedges and fresh parsley.

preparation time 20 minutes
cooking time 50 minutes
(plus standing time)
serves 4
nutritional count per serving 44.4g total fat (9.5g saturated fat); 3164kJ (757 cal); 43.6g carbohydrate; 43.2g protein; 6.2g fibre

lebanese-spiced drumsticks with baba ghanoush

sticky drumsticks with roasted root vegetables

1 medium sweet potato (400g), cut into wedges
300g salad potatoes, cut into wedges
1 large parsnip (350g), cut into wedges
2 tablespoons olive oil
3 cloves garlic, crushed
1 tablespoon chopped fresh rosemary
20 chicken drumsticks (1.4kg)
1½ teaspoons sweet paprika
1 tablespoon coarse cooking salt
2 teaspoons caster sugar
½ teaspoon ground black pepper
½ teaspoon ground lemon myrtle
¼ teaspoon ground cinnamon
2 tablespoons maple syrup

1 Preheat oven to 220°C/200°C fan-assisted.
2 Combine vegetables, oil, garlic and rosemary in large shallow baking dish. Roast, uncovered, in single layer, about 35 minutes or until vegetables are just tender.
3 Meanwhile, combine drumsticks and remaining ingredients in large bowl. Place drumsticks, in single layer, on oiled wire rack in large shallow baking dish; roast, uncovered, with vegetables about 30 minutes or until cooked through.
4 Serve drumsticks with roasted vegetables.

preparation time 20 minutes
cooking time 35 minutes
serves 4
nutritional count per serving 30.5g total fat (7.7g saturated fat); 2483kJ (594 cal); 40.0g carbohydrate; 38.2g protein; 4.9g fibre

glazed turkey with orange stuffing

4.5kg turkey
2 medium oranges (480g),
unpeeled, chopped coarsely
1 cup (250ml) water
2 cups (500ml) chicken stock
½ cup (125ml) bourbon
50g butter, melted
½ cup (175g) honey
2 tablespoons orange juice
2 tablespoons plain flour

orange stuffing
20g butter
1 large onion (200g), chopped
finely
4 cups (280g) stale breadcrumbs
1 cup (120g) coarsely chopped
toasted pecans
1 tablespoon finely grated
orange rind
2 tablespoons orange juice
½ cup (125ml) water
40g butter, melted
2 eggs, beaten lightly

1 Preheat oven to 180°C/160°C fan-assisted.
2 Discard neck from turkey. Rinse turkey under cold water; pat dry inside and out with absorbent paper. Tuck wings under turkey; fill large cavity with orange, tie legs together with kitchen string.
3 Place the water, stock and bourbon into large baking dish; place turkey on oiled wire rack over dish. Brush turkey with butter; cover with oiled foil. Roast 2 hours 10 minutes. Brush with half of the combined honey and juice. Roast, uncovered, 50 minutes or until cooked through, brushing often with remaining honey mixture. Remove turkey from dish; cover, stand 20 minutes.
4 Meanwhile, make orange stuffing.
5 Strain pan juices into large jug. Skim off 2 tablespoons of the oil; return oil to dish. Add flour; cook, stirring, until browned. Add juices; cook, stirring, until gravy boils and thickens. Strain gravy; serve with turkey.

orange stuffing melt butter in medium frying pan; cook onion, stirring, until soft. Combine onion in medium bowl with remaining ingredients. Roll rounded tablespoons into balls; place on oiled tray. Roast 20 minutes.

preparation time 30 minutes
cooking time 3 hours
serves 8
nutritional count per serving 60.7g total fat (19.5g saturated fat); 4619kJ (1105 cal); 58.8g carbohydrate; 69.7g protein; 4.4g fibre

roast turkey with sausage stuffing

4kg whole turkey
2 tablespoons olive oil
3 cups (750ml) chicken stock
40g butter
¼ cup (35g) plain flour
¼ cup (60ml) sweet sherry

sausage stuffing
1 tablespoon olive oil
1 small onion (80g), chopped finely
2 trimmed celery stalks (200g), chopped finely
2 rashers rindless bacon (130g), chopped finely
250g Italian sausages
4 cups (280g) stale breadcrumbs

2 teaspoons finely grated lemon rind
2 teaspoons lemon juice
2 tablespoons finely chopped fresh flat-leaf parsley
1 egg, beaten lightly

1 Make sausage stuffing. Preheat oven to 180°C/160°C fan-assisted.

2 Discard neck from turkey. Rinse turkey under cold running water; pat dry inside and out with absorbent paper. Fill neck cavity loosely with stuffing, secure skin over opening with toothpicks; fill large cavity loosely with stuffing.

Tie legs with kitchen string; tuck wings under turkey.

3 Place turkey on oiled wire rack in large flameproof baking dish. Brush turkey with oil; add 1 cup of the stock to dish. Cover with two layers of oiled foil; roast 2½ hours. Uncover; brush with pan juices. Roast, uncovered, 30 minutes or until browned all over and cooked through. Remove turkey from dish, cover; stand 20 minutes. Remove and discard toothpicks.

4 Drain pan juices from dish into large jug; skim and discard fat.

5 Melt butter in same dish over heat; cook flour, stirring, until mixture bubbles and thickens. Gradually add sherry, remaining stock and reserved pan juices; stir until it boils and thickens. Strain into same jug to serve.

sausage stuffing heat oil in medium frying pan; cook onion, celery and bacon, stirring, until onion softens. Squeeze sausage meat into large bowl; discard casings. Stir in onion mixture and remaining ingredients.

preparation time 20 minutes
cooking time 3 hours
(plus standing time)
serves 8
nutritional count per serving 56.5g total fat (17.9g saturated fat); 3816kJ (913 cal); 29.4g carbohydrate; 69.7g protein; 2.3g fibre

20g butter, melted
1 tablespoon honey
1 teaspoon light soy sauce
3.5kg whole goose
1 tablespoon plain flour

fruit & nut stuffing
2 tablespoons vegetable oil
200g chicken giblets, chopped finely
1 medium onion (150g), chopped finely
1 trimmed celery stalk (100g), chopped finely
1 medium apple (150g), chopped finely
½ cup (80g) coarsely chopped brazil nuts
½ cup (70g) slivered almonds
½ cup (75g) coarsely chopped dried apricots
½ cup (85g) finely chopped raisins
1 tablespoon chopped fresh mint leaves
1½ cups (100g) stale breadcrumbs

1 Preheat oven to 200°C/180°C fan-assisted.
2 Make fruit & nut stuffing.
3 Combine butter, honey and sauce in small bowl, brush mixture inside and outside of goose. Fill goose with stuffing, secure opening with skewers. Tie legs together, tuck wings under goose. Prick skin to release fat during roasting.

4 Lightly flour large oven bag; place goose in bag, secure with tie provided. Make holes in bag as advised on package. Place goose breast-side up in baking dish, cover dish with foil; roast 1 hour. Remove foil, roast goose further 1 hour. Remove and discard skewers.

fruit & nut stuffing Heat half the oil in medium saucepan; cook giblets, stirring, until browned; drain on absorbent paper. Add remaining oil to pan; cook onion and celery, stirring, until onion is soft.

Add apple and nuts; cook, stirring, until nuts are browned lightly. Remove from heat, stir in giblets, apricots, raisins, mint and breadcrumbs; cool.

preparation time 1 hour
cooking time 2 hours 15 minutes
serves 8
nutritional count per serving 113.0g total fat (32.2g saturated fat); 5405kJ (1293 cal); 27.0g carbohydrate; 43.4g protein; 4.3g fibre

roast goose with fruit & nut stuffing

Muscat is a sweet, aromatic dessert wine, possessing an almost musty flavour. It is made from the fully matured muscatel grape.

4 quails (780g)
1 medium lemon (140g)
20g butter
4 rashers rindless bacon (260g)
⅓ cup (80ml) muscat
250g green beans
½ cup (125ml) chicken stock
150g fresh muscatel grapes, halved

1 Preheat oven to 200°C/180°C fan-assisted.
2 Discard necks from quails. Wash quails under cold water; pat dry with absorbent paper.
3 Halve lemon; cut one lemon half into four wedges. Place one lemon wedge and a quarter of the butter inside each quail. Tuck legs along body, wrapping tightly with bacon rasher to hold legs in place.

4 Place quails in medium flameproof baking dish; drizzle with combined 1 tablespoon of the muscat and juice of remaining lemon half. Roast, uncovered, about 25 minutes or until quails are browned and cooked through. Remove quails from dish; cover to keep warm.
5 Meanwhile, boil, steam or microwave beans until tender; drain. Cover to keep warm.
6 Return dish with pan liquid to heat, add remaining muscat and stock; stir until sauce boils and reduces to about ½ cup. Add grapes; stir until heated though. Serve quail on beans topped with muscat sauce.

preparation time 15 minutes
cooking time 30 minutes
serves 4
nutritional count per serving 23.8g total fat (8.8g saturated fat); 1676kJ (401 cal); 9.4g carbohydrate; 33.0g protein; 2.6g fibre

roast bacon-wrapped quail with muscat sauce

italian roasted quail with braised vegetables

8 quails (1.3kg)
8 slices prosciutto (120g)
20g butter
½ cup (125ml) dry white wine
2 baby fennel bulbs (260g), trimmed, sliced thinly
4 cloves garlic, unpeeled
1 large red pepper (350g), sliced thinly
2 medium courgettes (240g), halved lengthways, sliced thickly
½ cup (125ml) chicken stock
1 medium lemon (140g), cut into eight wedges
¼ cup (60ml) double cream
1 tablespoon fresh oregano leaves

1 Preheat oven to 200°C/180°C fan-assisted.
2 Discard necks from quails. Wash quails under cold water; pat dry inside and out with absorbent paper. Tuck legs along body; wrap tightly with prosciutto to hold legs in place.
3 Heat butter in large flameproof baking dish; cook quails, in batches, until browned all over.
4 Place wine in same dish; bring to the boil. Reduce heat; simmer, uncovered, until wine has reduced to 1 tablespoon. Add fennel, garlic, pepper, courgette and stock; return to the boil. Place quails on top of vegetables; roast, uncovered, in oven 20 minutes. Add lemon to dish; roast, uncovered, further 10 minutes or until quails are cooked through.

5 Remove quails and garlic from dish. When cool enough to handle, squeeze garlic from skins into dish; stir in cream and oregano.
6 Serve quails on the braised vegetables.

preparation time 15 minutes
cooking time 45 minutes
serves 4
nutritional count per serving 30.8g total fat (12.4g saturated fat); 2052kJ (491 cal); 6.9g carbohydrate; 39.1g protein; 4.2g fibre

marinated chilli poussins

8 fresh medium red chillies
8 cloves garlic, peeled
2 small onions (200g), chopped finely
⅓ cup (80ml) red wine vinegar
1 tablespoon ground cumin
2 tablespoons olive oil
4 medium ripe tomatoes (750g), quartered
4 x 500g poussins

1 Process chillies, garlic, onion, vinegar and cumin until almost smooth.
2 Heat oil in medium frying pan, add chilli mixture; bring to the boil, stirring.
3 Process tomatoes until smooth, add to pan; cook, stirring, until mixture boils. Reduce heat; simmer, uncovered, stirring, about 20 minutes or until thickened. Cool. Refrigerate half of the mixture.
4 Cut poussins in half, remove neck and backbone. Rub remaining chilli mixture over poussins. Cover; refrigerate 3 hours or overnight.
5 Preheat oven to 220°C/200°C fan-assisted.
6 Place poussins, skin-side up, on oiled wire rack in shallow baking dish; sprinkle with salt. Roast, uncovered, 30 minutes until tender.
7 Serve reserved chilli mixture at room temperature, with poussins.

preparation time 20 minutes (plus refrigeration time)
cooking time 1 hour (plus cooling time)
serves 8
nutritional count per serving 24.5g total fat (6.8g saturated fat); 1425kJ (341 cal); 3.6g carbohydrate; 26.0g protein; 2.0g fibre

roasted poussins with dill & walnut pesto & risoni salad

⅓ cup firmly packed fresh flat-leaf parsley leaves
½ cup firmly packed fresh dill sprigs
½ cup (50g) roasted walnuts, chopped coarsely
¼ cup (20g) finely grated parmesan cheese
¼ cup (60ml) lemon juice
¼ cup (60ml) olive oil
4 x 500g poussins
2 medium lemons (280g), quartered

risoni salad
1 cup (220g) risoni
6 slices pancetta (90g), chopped finely
⅓ cup (50g) roasted pine nuts
¼ cup finely chopped fresh basil
¼ cup finely chopped fresh flat-leaf parsley
2 tablespoons olive oil
1 tablespoon red wine vinegar

1 Preheat oven to 180°C/160°C fan-assisted.
2 Blend or process herbs, nuts, cheese and juice until combined. With motor operating, gradually add oil in thin, steady stream until pesto thickens slightly. Reserve 1 tablespoon of pesto for risoni salad.
3 Wash poussins under cold water. Discard necks; pat dry inside and out with absorbent paper. Loosen poussin skin; rub remaining pesto between skin and flesh and over outside of poussins. Place 2 lemon quarters in cavity of each poussin.

4 Place poussins on oiled wire rack over baking dish; roast, uncovered, 45 minutes or until cooked through. Remove from dish; discard pan juices.
5 Meanwhile, make risoni salad.
6 Serve poussins, halved lengthways, on salad.

risoni salad cook pasta in large saucepan of boiling water, uncovered, until just tender; drain. Cook pancetta in heated oiled small frying pan, stirring, 5 minutes or until crisp. Place pasta and pancetta in large bowl with nuts, herbs, oil, vinegar and reserved pesto; toss gently to combine.

preparation time 55 minutes
cooking time 45 minutes
serves 4
nutritional count per serving 85.1g total fat (18.9g saturated fat); 5029kJ (1203 cal); 40.3g carbohydrate; 65.5g protein; 5.5g fibre

rack over shallow baking dish. Grill 6 minutes or until skin is browned and crisp. Turn, cook a further 3 minutes or until cooked as desired. Stand 5 minutes.

5 Meanwhile, boil, steam or microwave gai lan until just tender; drain well.

6 Place reserved marinade in saucepan; bring to the boil. Reduce heat; simmer, uncovered 1 minute.

7 Place noodles in heatproof bowl, cover with boiling water. Stand for 2 minutes, then separate noodles with a fork; drain.

8 Serve duck on noodles and gai lan; drizzle with hot marinade.

6 duck breast fillets (950g)
½ cup (125ml) chinese cooking wine
½ cup (125ml) soy sauce
4cm piece fresh ginger (20g), grated
3 cloves garlic, crushed
1 tablespoon white sugar
2 fresh long red chillies, chopped
600g gai lan, chopped
450g thin fresh hokkien noodles

1 Score the skin and fat of duck breasts through to the flesh.

2 Place duck in large bowl with combined wine, soy sauce, ginger, garlic, sugar and chilli. Cover; refrigerate 1 hour.

3 Preheat the grill part of the oven to 240°C/220°C fan-assisted.

4 Drain duck from marinade; reserve marinade. Place duck breasts, skin-side up, on oiled wire

preparation time 30 minutes (plus refrigeration time)
cooking time 10 minutes (plus standing time)
serves 6
nutritional count per serving 13.5g total fat (4.8g saturated fat); 1693kJ (405 cal); 23.4g carbohydrate; 39.0g protein; 6.3g fibre

soy duck breasts with noodles

garlic roasted duck

A duck wing portion consists of the wing and part of the breast.

2 tablespoons fish sauce
4 cloves garlic, crushed
1 cup (250ml) red wine vinegar
1 large onion (200g), chopped coarsely
2 teaspoons juniper berries, bruised
2 teaspoons fennel seeds
4 duck wing portions (1.5kg)
2 tablespoons natural yogurt

1 Combine fish sauce, garlic, vinegar, onion, berries and seeds in medium bowl. Place duck in single layer in shallow dish; pour over vinegar mixture. Cover; refrigerate 3 hours or overnight.
2 Preheat oven to 180°C/160°C fan-assisted.

3 Remove duck from marinade; reserve marinade. Place duck, skin-side up, on oiled wire rack over baking dish; roast, uncovered, 45 minutes or until tender.
4 Place reserved marinade in small saucepan; simmer, uncovered, about 5 minutes or until slightly thickened, strain. Stir yogurt into sauce; serve with duck.

preparation time 15 minutes (plus refrigeration time)
cooking time 45 minutes
serves 4
nutritional count per serving 79.2g total fat (23.9g saturated fat); 3507kJ (839 cal); 3.8g carbohydrate; 29.8g protein; 1.3g fibre

salt and pepper duck with shallots & cucumber

2kg duck
1 tablespoon finely ground sichuan peppercorns
2 teaspoons sea salt
1 tablespoon groundnut oil
20g butter
16 shallots (400g)
1 cucumber (260g), sliced thickly
1 tablespoon oyster sauce
½ cup (125ml) chicken stock
¼ cup coarsely chopped fresh coriander

1 Preheat oven to 180°C/160°C fan-assisted.
2 Place duck, breast-side up, on oiled wire rack in baking dish; rub combined pepper and salt into duck breast. Roast, uncovered, 1½ hours. Remove duck from oven; increase oven temperature to 240°C/220°C fan-assisted.
3 Using metal skewer or fork, prick duck skin all over. Turn duck breast-side down; roast, uncovered, 15 minutes. Turn duck breast-side up; roast, uncovered, 20 minutes or until browned and cooked through.
4 Meanwhile, heat oil and butter in large frying pan; cook shallots, stirring, until softened. Add cucumber; cook, stirring, 2 minutes. Stir in combined sauce and stock; bring to the boil. Remove from heat; stir in coriander.
5 Cut duck into pieces, serve on shallot and cucumber mixture; sprinkle with fresh coriander, if desired.

preparation time 10 minutes
cooking time 2 hours 5 minutes
serves 4
nutritional count per serving 114.2g total fat (35.2g saturated fat); 4995kJ (1195 cal); 5.6g carbohydrate; 39.2g protein; 1.7g fibre

tip use courgette instead of cucumber, if you prefer.

680g jar morello cherries
½ cup (125ml) chicken stock
½ cup (125ml) port
1 cinnamon stick
3 whole cloves
1 clove garlic, crushed
4 duck legs (1.2kg), excess fat removed
2 small green apples (260g)
1 cup (100g) roasted walnuts, chopped coarsely
3 spring onions, sliced thinly
1 cup firmly packed fresh flat-leaf parsley leaves
2 tablespoons olive oil
1 tablespoon lemon juice

1 Preheat oven to 160°C/140°C fan-assisted.
2 Strain cherries over small bowl. Combine cherry juice with stock, port, cinnamon, cloves and garlic in large baking dish. Place duck on oiled wire rack over dish; cover tightly with oiled foil. Roast, covered, about 2 hours or until duck meat is tender.
3 Strain pan liquid into large jug; skim and discard fat. Reserve cherry sauce for serving.
4 Cut apples into thin slices; cut slices into matchstick-sized pieces. Place apple and pitted cherries in large bowl with nuts, onion, parsley, oil and lemon juice; toss gently to combine.
5 Serve duck with salad and reheated cherry sauce.

preparation time 40 minutes
cooking time 2 hours
serves 4
nutritional count per serving 30.5g total fat (3.6g saturated fat); 1977kJ (473 cal); 25.1g carbohydrate; 15.0g protein; 5.0g fibre

tip slice apples just before serving to prevent discolouration.

slow-roasted duck with sour cherry, apple & walnut salad

roast beef with yorkshire puddings & red wine gravy

40g butter
2 tablespoons wholegrain mustard
1 tablespoon port
1½ tablespoons worcestershire sauce
2kg piece boneless beef sirloin
1½ cups (375ml) water
1 cup (250ml) dry red wine
40g butter
2 tablespoons plain flour
1½ cups (375ml) beef stock

yorkshire puddings
1 cup (150g) plain flour
1 teaspoon salt
1 cup (250ml) milk
2 eggs

1 Preheat oven to 220°C/200°C fan-assisted.
2 Rub combined mustard, port and 1 tablespoon of sauce all over beef. Place beef on oiled wire rack in flameproof baking dish; pour combined water and ½ cup (125ml) of the wine into dish. Roast, uncovered, 10 minutes. Reduce oven temperature to 180°C/160°C fan-assisted; roast 45 minutes or until cooked as desired. Add water if pan juices evaporate.
3 Make batter for yorkshire puddings.
4 Transfer beef to a plate; cover to keep warm. Increase oven temperature to 240°C/220°C fan-assisted. Drain pan juices into small heatproof bowl; freeze 10 minutes. Scrape solidified fat from top of pan juices; reserve pan juices. Divide 2 tablespoons of the fat (if necessary, use olive oil) among two 12-hole mini muffin pans. Preheat pans in oven 3 minutes; make sure fat is very hot, then immediately divide batter among holes.

Bake for 15 minutes or until puddings are browned and risen.
5 Melt butter in same baking dish; cook flour, stirring, until mixture is well browned. Gradually stir in remaining wine then stock, remaining sauce and reserved pan juices; cook, stirring until gravy boils and thickens slightly. Strain into jug; serve with beef, yorkshire puddings and peas, if desired.

yorkshire puddings sift flour and salt into medium bowl. Whisk in combined milk and eggs until batter is smooth. Cover; stand 30 minutes.

preparation time 25 minutes
cooking time 1 hour 15 minutes
serves 6
nutritional count per serving 23.5g total fat (11.3g saturated fat); 2784kJ (666 cal); 24.8g carbohydrate; 79.7g protein; 1.4g fibre

beef & veal

beef fillet with chermoulla

700g piece beef eye fillet

chermoulla
2 tablespoons olive oil
¼ cup coarsely chopped fresh flat-leaf parsley
2 tablespoons coarsely chopped fresh coriander
2 teaspoons grated lemon rind
1 tablespoon lemon juice
2 teaspoons sweet paprika
1 teaspoon ground cumin
1 teaspoon ground coriander
1 teaspoon salt

1 Preheat oven to 200°C/180°C fan-assisted.
2 Combine ingredients for chermoulla in large bowl.
3 Tie beef with kitchen string at 2cm intervals to keep its shape. Coat beef all over with chermoulla.
4 Place beef on oiled wire rack in baking dish. Roast, uncovered, 30 minutes or until cooked as desired. Cover; stand 10 minutes. Remove string and slice.
5 Serve beef with lemon wedges, if desired.

preparation time 15 minutes
cooking time 30 minutes
(plus standing time)
serves 4
nutritional count per serving 19.4g total fat (5.7g saturated fat); 1359kJ (325 cal); 0.2g carbohydrate; 37.3g protein; 0.3g fibre

tip beef can be marinated for 2 hours, if preferred. It is best cooked close to serving.

Chermoula is a marinade used in North African cuisine which is often used to flavour fish or seafood, but can also be used on meats or vegetables. It is usually a mixture of various chopped herbs and spices, along with oil, lemon juice and salt, and sometimes contains pickled lemons and garlic.

1.2kg beef standing rib roast
¼ cup (60ml) olive oil
2 teaspoons cracked black
pepper
500g baby new potatoes
500g pumpkin (or butternut
squash), chopped coarsely
500g sweet potatoes, chopped
coarsely
½ cup (125ml) brandy
1½ cups (375ml) beef stock
1 tablespoon cornflour
¼ cup (60ml) water
1 tablespoon finely chopped
fresh chives

1 Preheat oven to 200°C/180°C
fan-assisted.
2 Brush beef with 1 tablespoon of
the oil; sprinkle with pepper. Heat
1 tablespoon of the oil in large
shallow flameproof baking dish;
cook beef, uncovered, over high
heat until browned all over. Place
dish in oven; roast, uncovered,
about 45 minutes or until cooked
as desired.

3 Meanwhile, heat remaining oil in
another large flameproof baking
dish; cook potatoes, stirring, over
high heat until browned lightly.
Add pumpkin and sweet potato;
roast, uncovered, in oven about
35 minutes or until vegetables are
browned.
4 Place beef on vegetables, cover;
return to oven to keep warm.
5 Drain pan juices from beef
baking dish into medium saucepan,
add brandy; bring to the boil. Stir
in stock and blended cornflour
and the water, stirring, until sauce

boils and thickens slightly. Stir in
chives; pour gravy into medium
heatproof jug.
6 Serve beef and vegetables
with sauce.

preparation time 20 minutes
cooking time 1 hour 30 minutes
serves 4
nutritional count per serving
30.5g total fat (9.2g saturated
fat); 3219kJ (770 cal); 40.9g
carbohydrate; 63.9g protein;
5.7g fibre

beef rib roast with roast vegetables

2kg beef standing rib roast
¼ cup (60ml) olive oil
sea salt flakes
2 teaspoons cracked pepper
600g small beetroot, scrubbed, trimmed
1kg potatoes
40g butter, chopped
⅔ cup (160ml) milk, warmed
⅓ cup (80ml) double cream, warmed
¼ cup finely grated fresh horseradish

1 Preheat oven to 220°C/200°C fan-assisted.

2 Tie beef with kitchen string at 2cm intervals. Brush beef with 1 tablespoon of the oil; sprinkle with salt and pepper. Toss beetroot in remaining oil; add to dish. Roast, uncovered, about 20 minutes.

3 Reduce oven temperature to 180°C/160°C fan-assisted; roast beef and beetroot, uncovered, further 1 hour or until beef is cooked as desired and beetroot are tender. Remove beef from dish; cover, stand 20 minutes. Continue roasting the beetroot for a further 15 minutes or until it is tender.

4 Meanwhile, boil, steam or microwave potatoes until tender; drain. Mash potatoes; push through a sieve or mouli into a large bowl. Stir in butter then gradually beat in warmed milk and cream.

5 Serve beef with roast beetroot, potato puree and horseradish.

preparation time 25 minutes
cooking time 1 hour 35 minutes (plus standing time)
serves 4
nutritional count per serving 59.0g total fat (25.6g saturated fat); 4644kJ (1111 cal); 39.9g carbohydrate; 101.8g protein; 7.3g fibre

beef rib roast with potato puree & roasted beetroot

roasted beef fillet with rosti & creamed mushrooms

2 tablespoons olive oil
800g beef eye fillet
1 large sweet potatao (500g)
2 large waxy potatoes (600g)
80g butter
2 tablespoons olive oil, extra
30g butter, extra
200g chestnut mushrooms, halved
200g enoki mushrooms, trimmed
150g oyster mushrooms, halved
200g crème fraîche
3 spring onions, sliced thinly
⅓ cup firmly packed fresh flat-leaf parsley leaves

1 Preheat oven to 200°C/180°C fan-assisted.
2 Heat oil in large shallow flameproof baking dish; cook beef, uncovered, until browned all over. Roast, uncovered, in oven about 35 minutes or until cooked as desired. Cover to keep warm.
3 Meanwhile, coarsely grate sweet potato and potatoes into large bowl. Using hands, squeeze out excess moisture from potato mixture; shape mixture into eight portions. Heat 10g of the butter and 1 teaspoon of the extra oil in medium frying pan; spread one portion of the potato mixture over base of pan, flatten with spatula to form a firm pancake-like rosti. Cook, uncovered, over medium heat until browned; invert rosti onto large plate then gently slide back into pan to cook other side.

Drain on absorbent paper; cover to keep warm. Repeat process with remaining butter, oil and potato mixture.
4 Heat extra butter in same cleaned pan; cook mushrooms, stirring, until just tender. Add crème fraîche; bring to the boil. Reduce heat; simmer, stirring, until sauce thickens slightly. Remove from heat; stir in onion and parsley.
5 Serve sliced beef with rosti and mushrooms.

preparation time 20 minutes
cooking time 45 minutes
serves 4
nutritional count per serving 69.9g total fat (34.1g saturated fat); 4080kJ (976 cal); 34.4g carbohydrate; 54.2g protein; 8.4g fibre

slow-roasted beef & garlic with mustard cream

18 baby onions (720g)
2.5kg piece beef chuck steak
2 tablespoons olive oil
½ cup (125ml) red wine
2 sprigs fresh thyme
2 bulbs garlic, tops removed
1 cup (250ml) beef stock

mustard cream
½ cup (120g) soured cream
2 tablespoons wholegrain mustard

1 Preheat oven to 120°C/100°C fan-assisted.

2 Place onions in heatproof bowl; cover with boiling water and stand for 5 minutes. Drain, peel away the skins.

3 Brush beef all over with oil; cook in heated large flameproof baking dish until browned all over. Add wine, simmer, uncovered, until reduced by half. Remove dish from heat; sprinkle beef with thyme.

4 Add garlic, peeled onions and stock to dish, cover tightly; roast 2½ hours. Uncover; baste meat with pan juices. Roast, uncovered, further 2 hours. Cover; stand 30 minutes before slicing.

5 Combine ingredients for mustard cream in small bowl.

6 Serve beef with onions, garlic, strained pan juices, mustard cream and steamed green beans, if desired.

preparation time 15 minutes
cooking time 4 hours 35 minutes (plus standing time)
serves 6
nutritional count per serving 33.5g total fat (14.1g saturated fat); 2876kJ (688 cal); 4.5g carbohydrate; 87.1g protein; 3.1g fibre

1.5kg piece beef silverside
⅓ cup (80ml) extra virgin olive oil
6 whole baby onions (150g)
3 medium courgettes (360g),
halved lengthways
6 medium plum tomatoes (450g),
halved
3 finger aubergines (180g),
halved lengthways
2 medium yellow peppers (400g),
quartered
2 tablespoons balsamic vinegar
2 tablespoons shredded
fresh basil
2 tablespoons chopped fresh
tarragon
1 tablespoon drained baby capers

1 Preheat oven to 200°C/180°C fan-assisted.
2 Rub beef with 2 teaspoons of the oil; sprinkle with salt and freshly ground black pepper. Heat 1 tablespoon of the oil in flameproof baking dish; cook beef until browned all over. Add onions to dish; roast, uncovered, in oven 20 minutes.
3 Place courgettes, tomato, aubergine and pepper around beef in dish; roast further 40 minutes or until beef is cooked as desired. Remove beef from dish, cover with foil; stand 10 minutes.
4 Increase oven temperature to 240°C/220°C fan-assisted; roast vegetables further 10 minutes or until browned and tender. Drizzle vegetables with combined remaining oil, vinegar, herbs and baby capers.
5 Serve thinly sliced beef with vegetable mixture.

preparation time 15 minutes
cooking time 1 hour 20 minutes (plus standing time)
serves 6
nutritional count per serving 24.6g total fat (7.0g saturated fat); 2006kJ (480 cal); 5.6g carbohydrate; 57.5g protein; 3.3g fibre

mediterranean roast beef & vegetables

1 large beef shank (2.5kg),
quartered crossways
2 tablespoons plain flour
2 tablespoons olive oil
2 x 425g cans crushed tomatoes
½ cup (125ml) dry white wine
½ cup (125ml) beef stock
¼ cup (70g) tomato paste
¼ cup finely chopped fresh
flat-leaf parsley
2 tablespoons finely chopped
fresh lemon thyme

1 Preheat oven to 180°C/160°C fan-assisted.
2 Toss shank pieces in flour; shake away excess. Heat oil in large frying pan; cook shank pieces, in batches, until browned and almost crunchy all over.
3 Place undrained tomatoes, wine, stock and paste in deep 5-litre baking dish; stir to combine.

Place shank pieces, one at a time, standing upright, in dish; roast, covered, about 2 hours or until tender.
4 Remove shanks from dish. When cool enough to handle, remove meat from bones. Discard bones; chop meat coarsely. Return meat to dish with tomato sauce; reheat if necessary. Stir in herbs just before serving.
5 Serve shanks with risotto, if desired.

preparation time 30 minutes
cooking time 2 hours
45 minutes
serves 6
nutritional count per serving 18.8g total fat (6.1g saturated fat); 1701kJ (407 cal); 8.5g carbohydrate; 46.4g protein; 2.4g fibre

tip ask your butcher to quarter the beef shank crossways so that the pieces will fit into the baking dish.

slow-roasted beef shank

sri lankan spicy beef ribs with coconut pilaf

1.6kg american-style spareribs (order in advance from butcher)
¼ cup (60ml) groundnut oil
¼ cup (60ml) white vinegar
1 teaspoon sambal oelek
1 teaspoon ground turmeric
4 cloves
½ teaspoon ground cardamom
3 cloves garlic, crushed
2 teaspoons grated fresh ginger
1 small onion (80g), chopped finely

coconut pilaf
40g butter
1 medium onion (150g), chopped coarsely
1 medium carrot (120g), chopped coarsely
2 cups (400g) basmati rice, washed, drained
1 litre (4 cups) chicken stock
¼ cup firmly packed fresh coriander leaves
¼ cup (10g) flaked coconut
¼ cup (40g) raisins

1 Using kitchen scissors, cut ribs into sections. Combine ribs in large bowl with combined remaining ingredients. Cover; refrigerate 3 hours or overnight.
2 Preheat oven to 240°C/220°C fan-assisted.
3 Drain ribs; reserve marinade. Place ribs on oiled wire rack over large shallow baking dish. Roast, uncovered, brushing frequently with reserved marinade, about 30 minutes or until browned and cooked through, turning once halfway through cooking time.
4 Meanwhile, make coconut pilaf; serve ribs on pilaf.

coconut pilaf heat butter in medium saucepan; cook onion and carrot, stirring, until onion softens. Add rice; cook, stirring, 1 minute. Add stock; bring to the boil. Reduce heat; simmer, covered, about 20 minutes or until rice is just tender. Remove from heat; fluff rice with fork. Stir in coriander, coconut and raisins, cover; stand 5 minutes before serving.

preparation time 20 minutes (plus refrigeration time)
cooking time 35 minutes (plus standing time)
serves 4
nutritional count per serving 35.9g total fat (14.5g saturated fat); 3775kJ (903 cal); 93.3g carbohydrate; 49.3g protein; 3.8g fibre

veal rack with roasted mushroom sauce

1kg veal rack
¼ cup (60ml) olive oil
1kg baby new potatoes
300g button mushrooms
150g shimeji or oyster
mushrooms
2 cloves garlic, sliced
2 tablespoons grated parmesan
cheese
2 tablespoons plain flour
1½ cups (375ml) chicken stock
⅓ cup (80ml) double cream
2 tablespoons chopped fresh
flat-leaf parsley

1 Preheat oven to 200°C/180°C fan-assisted.
2 Place veal on oiled wire rack in shallow flameproof medium baking dish. Rub veal with 1 tablespoon of the oil, sprinkle with sea salt flakes and freshly ground black pepper; roast for 10 minutes.
3 Place potatoes in small baking dish; roast potatoes alongside veal for further 30 minutes or until veal is cooked as desired, brushing with any pan juices. Remove veal from dish; cover to keep warm.
4 Combine mushrooms, garlic and remaining oil in veal baking dish; roast mushroom mixture alongside potatoes for further 20 minutes or until potatoes are tender. Sprinkle potatoes with cheese, then roast a further 5 minutes or until cheese is melted.
5 Meanwhile, place mushroom mixture in baking dish over medium heat, add flour; cook, stirring, about 2 minutes or until bubbling. Gradually stir in stock and any veal pan juices; cook, stirring, until sauce boils and thickens. Stir in cream and parsley until heated through.
6 Cut the veal into cutlets, serve with mushroom sauce and potatoes.

preparation time 20 minutes
cooking time 1 hour 5 minutes
serves 4
nutritional count per serving 29.0g total fat (10.0g saturated fat); 2792kJ (668 cal); 38.7g carbohydrate; 58.4g protein; 9.1g fibre

mustard-crusted rack of veal with sweet potato mash

2 tablespoons wholegrain mustard
3 spring onions, chopped finely
2 cloves garlic, crushed
1 tablespoon finely chopped fresh rosemary
2 tablespoons olive oil
1kg veal rack (8 cutlets), trimmed
2 small sweet potatoes (500g), chopped coarsely
20g butter
⅓ cup (80ml) double cream
1 large brown onion (200g), sliced thinly
400g mushrooms, sliced thinly
1 tablespoon plain flour
¼ cup (60ml) dry white wine
¾ cup (180ml) chicken stock
¼ cup coarsely chopped fresh flat-leaf parsley

1 Preheat oven to 200°C/180°C fan-assisted.
2 Combine mustard, spring onion, half of the garlic, rosemary and half of the oil in small jug. Place veal on oiled wire rack over large shallow flameproof baking dish; coat veal all over with mustard mixture. Roast, uncovered, about 30 minutes or until browned all over and cooked as desired. Cover to keep warm.
3 Meanwhile, boil, steam or microwave sweet potatoes until tender; drain. Mash sweet potato in large bowl with butter and half of the cream until smooth.

4 Heat remaining oil in same flameproof dish; cook brown onion and remaining garlic, stirring, until onion softens. Add mushrooms; cook, stirring, about 5 minutes or until just tender. Add flour; cook, stirring, until mixture bubbles and thickens. Gradually stir in wine and stock; stir until sauce boils and thickens. Add remaining cream and parsley; stir until heated through.
5 Serve veal with sweet potato mash and mushroom sauce.

preparation time 25 minutes
cooking time 35 minutes
serves 4
nutritional count per serving 27.4g total fat (11.2g saturated fat); 2370kJ (567 cal); 21.8g carbohydrate; 53.2g protein; 6.0g fibre

2 tablespoons olive oil
20g butter
2kg veal breast
2 medium onions (300g),
chopped coarsely
2 cloves garlic, quartered
2 medium carrots (240g),
chopped coarsely
4 trimmed celery stalks (400g),
chopped coarsely
6 sprigs fresh rosemary
1 cup (250ml) dry white wine
1 cup (250ml) beef stock

soft polenta
1.5 litres (6 cups) water
2 teaspoons salt
2 cups (340g) polenta
½ cup (125ml) milk
½ cup (40g) grated parmesan
cheese

1 Heat oil and butter in large flameproof baking dish; cook veal until browned all over, remove from dish.
2 Preheat oven to 160°C/140°C fan-assisted.
3 Cook onion and garlic in same dish, stirring, until soft. Stir in carrot, celery and rosemary; cook, stirring, until softened slightly. Add combined wine and stock; bring to the boil. Return veal to dish, cover tightly; roast in oven about 3 hours or until tender.

4 Make soft polenta.
5 Serve veal slices with soft polenta; top with vegetables and drizzle with pan juices.

soft polenta bring the water and salt to the boil in large saucepan. Gradually stir in polenta then simmer, uncovered, about 25 minutes or until thick, stirring constantly. Add milk; cook, stirring, about 5 minutes or until mixture is thick. Stir in cheese.

preparation time 20 minutes
cooking time 3 hours
20 minutes
serves 8
nutritional count per serving
13.6g total fat (4.6g saturated fat);
2266kJ (542 cal); 34.3g
carbohydrate; 63.1g protein;
3.3g fibre

slow-roasted veal breast with soft polenta

spring roast lamb with mint sauce

2 tablespoons extra virgin olive oil
4 cloves garlic, crushed
2 tablespoons lemon juice
2 tablespoons fresh oregano
leaves
2kg boned leg lamb
1kg desiree potatoes, cut into
wedges
1 cup (250ml) chicken stock
2 sprigs fresh rosemary

mint sauce
2 cups firmly packed fresh mint
leaves
2 tablespoons ground almonds
2 cloves garlic, quartered
⅓ cup (80ml) extra virgin olive oil
2 tablespoons lemon juice

1 Combine oil, garlic, juice and oregano in small bowl. Rub lamb all over with garlic mixture, inside and out. Cover; refrigerate 3 hours or overnight.

2 Preheat oven to 200°C/180°C fan-assisted.

3 Place potatoes in large oiled baking dish. Pour stock over potatoes; top with rosemary sprigs. Place lamb on top of potatoes. Roast, uncovered, about 1 hour or until lamb is cooked as desired. Remove lamb from dish; cover, stand 15 minutes.

4 Increase oven temperature to 240°C/230°C fan-assisted; roast potatoes further 15 minutes or until browned.

5 Make mint sauce.

6 Serve lamb with potatoes and sauce, and red coleslaw, if desired.

mint sauce blend or process mint, ground almonds and garlic until finely chopped. Transfer mixture to small bowl; stir in oil and lemon juice.

preparation time 20 minutes (plus refrigeration time)
cooking time 1 hour 15 minutes
serves 6
nutritional count per serving 38.4g total fat (10.8g saturated fat); 3114kJ (745 cal); 19.3g carbohydrate; 78.7g protein; 4.1g fibre

lamb

roasted spiced lamb & vegetables

2 x 350g mini lamb roasts
1 tablespoon olive oil
250g cherry tomatoes
2 medium courgettes (240g),
halved lengthways
250g baby red peppers or 1 large
red pepper (350g), quartered

spice rub
2 tablespoons olive oil
1 teaspoon dried oregano leaves
3 cloves garlic, crushed
¼ teaspoon salt
1 teaspoon sweet paprika
1 tablespoon lemon juice

1 Preheat oven to very hot
(240°C/220°C fan-assisted).
2 Combine ingredients for spice
rub in small bowl; rub half of the
spice rub over lamb.
3 Heat oil in medium flameproof
baking dish; cook lamb, over heat,
until browned all over. Roast,
uncovered, in oven for 10 minutes.
4 Combine remaining spice
rub with vegetables in medium
baking dish; roast alongside lamb
15 minutes. Remove lamb; cover,
stand 10 minutes.
5 Roast vegetables further
5 minutes or until tender.
6 Serve lamb with vegetables.

preparation time 15 minutes
cooking time 35 minutes
serves 4
nutritional count per serving
29.5g total fat (8.9g saturated
fat); 1852kJ (443 cal); 4.9g
carbohydrate; 38.7g protein;
3.1g fibre

4 sprigs fresh rosemary

2kg leg of lamb

2 cloves garlic, each cut into
8 slices

¼ cup (60ml) olive oil

40g butter

1 small onion (80g), chopped
finely

2 tablespoons plain flour

½ cup (125ml) dry red wine

1¼ cups (375ml) lamb or beef
stock

1 Preheat oven to 220°C/200°C fan-assisted.

2 Cut 16 similar-size rosemary sprigs from bunch; place remainder of bunch in large flameproof baking dish.

3 Remove and discard as much excess fat from lamb as possible. Using sharp knife, pierce lamb about 16 times all over; press garlic slices and rosemary sprigs into cuts. Place lamb on top of rosemary in baking dish. Pour oil over lamb; roast, uncovered, 20 minutes.

4 Reduce oven temperature to 180°C/160°C fan-assisted; roast lamb, further 1½ hours, occasionally basting with pan juices. Remove lamb from dish; stand 5 minutes.

5 Drain juices from dish, melt butter in pan over low heat; cook onion, stirring, until soft. Stir in flour; cook, stirring, about 5 minutes or until browned. Pour in wine and stock; cook over high heat, stirring, until gravy boils and thickens. Strain, then serve with lamb.

preparation time 10 minutes
cooking time 2 hours
serves 6
nutritional count per serving 28.1g total fat (10.9g saturated fat); 2119kJ (507 cal); 3.9g carbohydrate; 56.0g protein; 0.5g fibre

tip we used red shiraz in this recipe but any dry red wine can be used.

roast leg of lamb with gravy

crusted lamb racks & potato wedges

5 medium potatoes (1kg),
cut into wedges
¼ cup (60ml) olive oil
4 x 4 french-trimmed cutlet lamb
racks (600g)
½ teaspoon dried chilli flakes
2 tablespoons kalonji seeds
2 tablespoons sesame seeds
1 clove garlic, crushed
½ cup loosely packed fresh
flat-leaf parsley leaves

1 Preheat oven to 200°C/180°C fan-assisted.
2 Combine potato with 2 tablespoons of the oil on oven tray. Roast potato, in single layer, uncovered, about 55 minutes or until browned lightly and crisp.
3 Meanwhile, place lamb on separate oven tray; rub all over with combined remaining oil, chilli, seeds and garlic. Roast, uncovered, for last 20 minutes of potato cooking time or until lamb is browned and cooked as desired.

4 Combine potatoes and parsley in large bowl; serve with lamb and lemon, if desired.

preparation time 15 minutes
cooking time 55 minutes
serves 4
nutritional count per serving 31.6g total fat (8.4g saturated fat); 2044kJ (489 cal); 28.9g carbohydrate; 22.4g protein; 4.8g fibre

garlic & sage lamb racks

3 large red onions (900g)
12 fresh sage leaves
⅓ cup (80ml) olive oil
2 tablespoons coarsely chopped fresh sage
4 cloves garlic, chopped coarsely
4 x 4 french-trimmed cutlet lamb racks (600g)

1 Preheat oven to 220°C/200°C fan-assisted.
2 Halve onions, slice into thin wedges; place in large baking dish with sage leaves and half of the oil.
3 Combine remaining oil in small bowl with chopped sage and garlic. Press sage mixture all over lamb; place on onion in dish.
4 Roast, uncovered, for about 25 minutes or until lamb is browned all over and cooked as desired. Cover lamb racks; stand 10 minutes.

preparation time 10 minutes
cooking time 25 minutes (plus standing time)
serves 4

nutritional count per serving 31.3g fat (8.5g saturated fat); 1676kJ (401 cal); 12.4g carbohydrate; 18.4g protein; 3.4g fibre

lamb with aioli

⅓ cup (80ml) olive oil
6 sprigs fresh thyme
900g large potatoes
6 x 4 extra-trimmed cutlet
lamb racks (900g)
500g spinach, trimmed
20g butter
1 clove garlic, crushed
250g chestnut mushrooms,
sliced thickly
1 tablespoon balsamic vinegar

aïoli

½ teaspoon dijon mustard
1 tablespoon white wine vinegar
1 clove garlic, crushed
2 egg yolks
¾ cup (180ml) extra virgin
olive oil
2 teaspoons lemon juice

1 Heat oil in small saucepan;
deep-fry thyme briefly, about
5 seconds or until fragrant.
Remove thyme from oil, drain on
absorbent paper; reserve oil.
2 Preheat oven to 200°C/180°C
fan-assisted.
3 Cut potatoes into 1cm slices.
Heat 2 tablespoons of the
reserved thyme oil in flameproof
baking dish; cook potato slices, in
batches, until lightly browned both
sides. Return all potato to same
baking dish.
4 Add lamb to baking dish;
roast, uncovered, in oven about
15 minutes or until cooked as
desired. Cover to keep warm.
5 Meanwhile, make aïoli.
6 Boil, steam or microwave
spinach until just wilted; drain.

7 Heat remaining thyme oil with
butter in small saucepan; cook
garlic and mushrooms, stirring,
until mushrooms soften.
8 Cut lamb racks into cutlets;
divide among serving plates with
spinach, potato and mushrooms.
Top with aïoli, garnish with fried
thyme; drizzle with vinegar.

aïoli whisk mustard, vinegar,
garlic and egg yolks in small bowl
until combined. Gradually add oil
in thin, steady stream, whisking
constantly, until aïoli thickens.
Whisk in lemon juice.

preparation time 35 minutes
cooking time 30 minutes
serves 6
nutritional count per serving
51.4g total fat (11.3g saturated
fat); 2700kJ (646 cal); 20.2g
carbohydrate; 24.2g protein;
5.4g fibre

8 fresh small red thai chillies, chopped coarsely

4 cloves garlic, quartered

1 teaspoon salt

2 tablespoons coriander seeds

1 tablespoon cumin seeds

2 teaspoons caraway seeds

1 tablespoon coarsely grated lemon rind

1 tablespoon lemon juice

¼ cup (60ml) olive oil

2 x 6 cutlet lamb racks (450g)

⅓ cup (80ml) olive oil, extra

8 saffron threads

2 cups (400g) couscous

20g butter, chopped

2 cups (500ml) boiling water

2 tablespoons finely chopped rinsed preserved lemon

100g cracked green olives, chopped coarsely

¼ cup fresh mint leaves, shredded finely

½ cup (70g) slivered almonds, roasted

200g sheep's-milk yogurt

1 Preheat oven to 240°C/220°C fan-assisted.

2 Blend or process chilli, garlic, salt, seeds, rind, juice and oil until mixture forms a paste.

3 Cut slits between cutlets with sharp knife; push 1 teaspoon of the harissa paste in each slit, press remaining harissa over outside of racks. Place racks in large oiled baking dish; roast, uncovered, 35 minutes or until browned and cooked as desired. Cover racks; stand 5 minutes before slicing into cutlets.

4 Meanwhile, heat extra oil in small saucepan; stir in saffron. Remove from heat, cool; strain through fine strainer into small jug.

5 Combine couscous, butter and the water in large heatproof bowl; fluff with fork to separate grains. Stir in lemon, olives, mint and almonds.

6 Serve cutlets with couscous and yogurt; drizzle with saffron oil.

preparation time 20 minutes
cooking time 35 minutes
serves 4
nutritional count per serving 54.7g total fat (11.8g saturated fat); 4042kJ (967 cal); 86.5g carbohydrate; 30.6g protein; 4.1g fibre

lamb cutlets in harissa with couscous

A duxelles (doo-zell) is a classic French mixture of finely chopped shallots and mushrooms cooked in butter, often used in pâtés and stuffings.

Cut potatoes into wedges. Place vegetables, in single layer, in large shallow flameproof baking dish; drizzle with oil.

4 Place lamb on oiled wire rack over vegetables; roast, uncovered, about 1½ hours or until lamb is cooked as desired and vegetables are tender. Remove lamb and vegetables from dish, cover lamb; stand 10 minutes.

5 Meanwhile, place dish containing juices over heat; stir in stock and remaining vinegar, bring to the boil. Strain sauce into small jug.

6 Serve lamb with vegetables, drizzled with sauce.

40g butter
1 clove garlic, crushed
3 shallots (75g), chopped finely
150g chestnut mushrooms, chopped finely
½ cup (125ml) balsamic vinegar
1.2kg easy-carve leg of lamb
1 teaspoon sea salt
2 large parsnips (700g)
2 large carrots (360g)
1 large sweet potato (500g)
2 large potatoes (600g)
2 tablespoons olive oil
½ cup (125ml) beef stock

1 Melt butter in large frying pan; cook garlic, shallots and mushrooms, stirring, until shallot softens. Add half of the vinegar; bring to the boil. Reduce heat; simmer duxelles, uncovered, about 5 minutes or until liquid has evaporated. Fill lamb cavity with duxelles; rub lamb all over with salt.

2 Preheat oven to 180°C/160°C fan-assisted.

3 Halve parsnips, carrots and sweet potato first crossways, then lengthways; cut into thick slices.

preparation time 30 minutes
cooking time 1 hour 45 minutes
serves 4
nutritional count per serving 34.3g total fat (13.9g saturated fat); 3432kJ (821 cal); 50.5g carbohydrate; 76.5g protein; 11.0g fibre

duxelles stuffed lamb with roast veg

traditional roast lamb dinner

2kg leg of lamb
3 sprigs fresh rosemary, chopped coarsely
½ teaspoon sweet paprika
1kg potatoes, chopped coarsely
500g piece pumpkin (or butternut squash), chopped coarsely
3 small onions (240g), halved
2 tablespoons olive oil
2 tablespoons plain flour
1 cup (250ml) chicken stock
¼ cup (60ml) dry red wine

preparation time 30 minutes
cooking time 1 hour 10 minutes
serves 6

nutritional count per serving
20.1g total fat (7.1g saturated fat); 2316kJ (554 cal); 28.5g carbohydrate; 60.9g protein; 3.8g fibre

1 Preheat oven to 200°C/180°C fan-assisted.

2 Place lamb in large oiled baking dish; using sharp knife, score skin at 2cm intervals, sprinkle with rosemary and paprika. Roast, uncovered, 15 minutes. Reduce oven temperature to 180°C/160°C fan-assisted; roast, uncovered, further 45 minutes or until cooked as desired.

3 Meanwhile, place potato, pumpkin and onion, in single layer, in large shallow baking dish; drizzle with oil. Roast, uncovered, alongside lamb for last 45 minutes of lamb cooking time. Remove lamb and vegetables from oven; cover to keep warm.

4 Strain pan juices from lamb dish into medium jug. Return ¼ cup of the pan juices to flameproof dish over medium heat, add flour; cook, stirring, 5 minutes or until mixture bubbles and browns. Gradually stir in stock and wine; cook over high heat, stirring, until gravy boils and thickens. Strain.

5 Serve sliced lamb with roasted vegetables and gravy and, if desired, cauliflower cheese.

51

greek roast lamb with skordalia & lemon-scented potatoes

Skordalia is a Greek sauce made with garlic and thickened with potatoes, nuts, or bread. We use potatoes as a base in our recipe.

2kg leg of lamb
2 cloves garlic, crushed
½ cup (125ml) lemon juice
2 tablespoons olive oil
1 tablespoon fresh oregano leaves
1 teaspoon fresh lemon thyme leaves
5 large potatoes (1.5kg), cut into 3cm pieces
2 tablespoons olive oil, extra
1 tablespoon finely grated lemon rind
2 tablespoons lemon juice
1 teaspoon fresh lemon thyme leaves

skordalia
1 medium potato (200g), quartered
3 cloves garlic, quartered
1 tablespoon lemon juice
1 tablespoon white wine vinegar
2 tablespoons water
⅓ cup (80ml) olive oil
1 tablespoon warm water

1 Combine lamb with garlic, juice, oil, oregano and thyme in large bowl. Cover; refrigerate 3 hours or overnight.
2 Preheat oven to 160°C/140°C fan-assisted. Place lamb in large baking dish; roast, uncovered, 4 hours.
3 Meanwhile, make skordalia. Toss potato in large bowl with combined remaining ingredients; place, in single layer, on oven tray. Cook potato, uncovered, for last 30 minutes of lamb cooking time.
4 Remove lamb from oven; cover to keep warm. Increase oven temperature to 220°C/200°C fan-assisted; roast potatoes, uncovered, 20 minutes or until crisp and tender. Serve potatoes and lamb with skordalia.

skordalia boil, steam or microwave potato until tender; drain. Push potato through food mill or fine sieve into large bowl; cool 10 minutes. Add garlic, juice, vinegar and the water to potato; stir until well combined. Place potato mixture in blender; with motor operating, gradually add oil in a thin, steady stream, only until skordalia thickens (do not overmix). Stir in the water.

preparation time 40 minutes (plus refrigeration time)
cooking time 4 hours 20 minutes (plus cooling time)
serves 4
nutritional count per serving 57.0g total fat (14.0g saturated fat); 4556kJ (1090 cal); 51.5g carbohydrate; 91.2g protein; 6.7g fibre

slow-roasted lamb leg with artichokes & lemon

½ cup coarsely chopped fresh flat-leaf parsley

½ cup (75g) pitted kalamata (Greek) olives, quartered

4 drained anchovy fillets

4 cloves garlic, quartered

2 teaspoons finely grated lemon rind

2 tablespoons lemon juice

2 tablespoons drained capers, rinsed

2 tablespoons olive oil

2kg leg of lamb

800g jerusalem artichokes, halved lengthways

2 small red onions (200g), cut into wedges

2 medium lemons (280g), cut into wedges

12 cloves garlic, unpeeled

1 Preheat oven to 150ºC/130ºC fan-assisted.

2 Blend or process parsley, olives, anchovies, quartered garlic, rind, juice, capers and 1 tablespoon of the oil until mixture is chopped coarsely.

3 Using sharp knife, pierce lamb down to the bone at 3cm intervals along the length of the leg. Spread olive mixture all over lamb, pressing into cuts.

4 Combine artichokes, onion, lemon, unpeeled garlic and remaining oil in large shallow baking dish. Place lamb on artichoke mixture; cover tightly with foil. Roast, uncovered, 4 hours.

5 Serve lamb with vegetable mixture.

preparation time 30 minutes
cooking time 4 hours
serves 4
nutritional count per serving 30.4g total fat (10.4g saturated fat); 2888kJ (691 cal); 14.6g carbohydrate; 87.8g protein; 8.7g fibre

¼ teaspoon ground turmeric

2 teaspoons cumin seeds, crushed

1 teaspoon ground coriander

2 teaspoons finely grated lemon rind

2 tablespoons lemon juice

2 cloves garlic, crushed

1 tablespoon honey, warmed

1 teaspoon salt

1.5kg easy carve leg of lamb

2 cups (500ml) water

coconut rice

1½ cups (300g) basmati rice

400ml coconut milk

1½ cups (375ml) chicken stock

4 fresh dates, sliced thinly

¼ cup (35g) slivered almonds, roasted

80g baby spinach leaves

1 Dry-fry turmeric, cumin and coriander in small frying pan, stirring, about 1 minute or until fragrant. Combine spices, rind, juice, garlic, honey and salt in small bowl. Place lamb in shallow baking tray; rub or brush spice mixture all over lamb. Cover; refrigerate several hours or overnight.

2 Preheat oven to 180°C/160°C fan-assisted.

3 Place lamb on oiled wire rack in medium baking dish; pour the water into dish. Roast, uncovered, about 1 hour 10 minutes or until lamb is cooked as desired. Cover; stand 15 minutes. Skim fat from pan juices.

4 Meanwhile, make coconut rice.

5 Serve lamb and juices with rice.

coconut rice place rice in large bowl, fill with cold water and stir with hand. Drain, repeat process two to three times or until water runs clear. Drain rice in sieve. Place drained rice, coconut milk and stock in medium saucepan; cover, bring to the boil. Reduce heat; simmer, covered tightly, over low heat 12 minutes or until liquid is absorbed. Remove from heat. Stir in dates, almonds and spinach.

preparation time 20 minutes (plus refrigeration time)
cooking time 1 hour 10 minutes
serves 6
nutritional count per serving 27.6g total fat (16.9g saturated fat); 2721kJ (651 cal); 50.9g carbohydrate; 47.9g protein; 3.2g fibre

spiced roast lamb with coconut rice

1 medium red pepper (200g)
700g boned loin of lamb
2 cloves garlic, crushed
20g baby spinach leaves
⅓ cup loosely packed fresh basil leaves
1 tablespoon olive oil

tomato concasse

1 tablespoon olive oil
3 shallots (75g), chopped finely
4 cloves garlic, crushed
1.2kg large plum tomatoes, peeled, deseeded, chopped finely
2 tablespoons red wine vinegar

1 Preheat oven to 240°C/220°C fan-assisted.

2 Make tomato concasse.

3 Meanwhile, quarter pepper; discard seeds and membranes. Roast in oven, skin-side up, until skin blisters and blackens. Cover pepper in cling film or paper for 5 minutes; peel away skin, slice flesh thinly.

4 Reduce oven temperature to 180°C/160°C fan-assisted.

5 Place lamb, cut-side up, on board; rub garlic into lamb then place pepper, spinach and basil down centre of lamb; roll tightly, secure at 2cm intervals with kitchen string. Rub oil over lamb roll.

6 Place lamb on oiled wire rack over large shallow baking dish; roast, uncovered, about 1 hour or until lamb is browned and cooked as desired. Cover to keep warm.

7 Serve thickly sliced lamb with concasse and, if desired, peas.

tomato concasse heat oil in medium saucepan; cook shallot and garlic, stirring, until shallot softens. Add tomato and vinegar; cook, covered, over low heat, 15 minutes. Uncover; simmer, stirring occasionally, 30 minutes or until mixture thickens slightly.

preparation time 30 minutes
cooking time 1 hour 30 minutes (plus standing time)
serves 4
nutritional count per serving 20.3g total fat (7.7g saturated fat); 1526kJ (365 cal); 5.0g carbohydrate; 39.1g protein; 3.1g fibre

rolled lamb loin with tomato concasse

chilli & honey-glazed lamb loin with mee goreng

Mee goreng is a dish of spicy fried noodles with vegetables, and is popular in Indonesia, Singapore and Malaysia.

800g boned and rolled lamb loin
1 tablespoon sambal oelek
1 tablespoon honey
1 tablespoon kecap manis

mee goreng
10 dried shiitake mushrooms
450g hokkien noodles
2 teaspoons groundnut oil
1cm piece fresh ginger (5g), grated
1 clove garlic, crushed
1 spring onion, sliced thinly
100g mangetout, sliced thinly
1 teaspoon sambal oelek
2 tablespoons kecap manis
1 tablespoon hoisin sauce
1 tablespoon oyster sauce
⅓ cup (80ml) beef stock

1 Preheat oven to 180°C/160°C fan-assisted.
2 Place lamb on oiled wire rack over baking dish; brush with combined remaining ingredients. Roast, uncovered, 30 minutes. Cover lamb; roast further 15 minutes or until cooked as desired. Cover lamb; stand 10 minutes.
3 Meanwhile, make mee goreng; serve with sliced lamb.

mee goreng place mushrooms in small heatproof bowl, cover with boiling water; stand 20 minutes or until tender, drain. Slice mushrooms thinly. Place noodles in large heatproof bowl; cover with boiling water, separate with fork, drain. Heat oil in wok; stir-fry ginger and garlic until fragrant. Add mushrooms and noodles to wok; stir-fry 2 minutes. Add remaining ingredients; stir-fry until mangetout are just tender.

preparation time 20 minutes
cooking time 45 minutes
serves 4
nutritional count per serving 21.5g total fat (9.1g saturated fat); 2926kJ (700 cal); 70.2g carbohydrate; 55.4g protein; 3.6g fibre

slow-roasted lamb shoulder

2 tablespoons olive oil
1.2kg lamb shoulder
2 medium onions (300g), chopped coarsely
2 medium carrots (240g), chopped coarsely
2 trimmed celery stalks (200g), chopped coarsely
1 tablespoon white sugar
½ cup (125ml) dry red wine
½ cup (125ml) lamb stock
10 sprigs fresh oregano

1 Preheat oven to 150°C/130°C fan-assisted.
2 Heat oil in large flameproof baking dish; cook lamb, uncovered, over high heat until browned all over. Remove lamb from dish.
3 Cook onion, carrot and celery in same dish, stirring, until browned lightly. Add sugar; cook, stirring, 1 minute. Add wine and stock; bring to the boil, then remove from heat.
4 Place half of the oregano on vegetables; place lamb on top, then place remaining oregano on lamb. Roast, covered tightly, 1½ hours. Turn lamb; roast, covered, another 1½ hours. Turn again; roast, covered, further 1 hour. Remove lamb from dish; cover with foil to keep warm.
5 Strain dish contents, discarding vegetables, oregano and as much fat as possible. Serve lamb with strained hot pan juices.

preparation time 15 minutes
cooking time 4 hours 15 minutes
serves 4
nutritional count per serving 29.1g total fat (10.4g saturated fat); 2149kJ (514 cal); 11.7g carbohydrate; 45.0g protein; 3.2g fibre

tip beef stock can be substituted for lamb stock, and rosemary can be substituted for oregano.

5 Spread lamb with half of the pesto. Roll from short side to enclose pesto; secure lamb with skewers, tie with kitchen string at 2cm intervals. Place lamb on oiled wire rack in large baking dish; spread remaining pesto all over lamb. Roast, uncovered, about 1¾ hours or until cooked as desired. Cover; stand 10 minutes. Remove and discard skewers.

⅓ cup (50g) unroasted hazelnuts
½ cup firmly packed fresh coriander leaves
⅓ cup firmly packed fresh basil leaves
4cm piece fresh ginger (20cm), grated
5 cloves garlic, crushed
2 tablespoons lime juice
2 teaspoons fish sauce
1 teaspoon brown sugar
2 tablespoons olive oil
1.7kg lamb shoulder, boned

1 Preheat oven to 200°C/180°C fan-assisted.
2 Spread nuts in single layer on oven tray; roast, uncovered, 5 minutes or until skins begin to flake. Rub nuts in soft cloth to remove skins; cool.
3 Reduce oven temperature to 180°C/160°C fan-assisted.
4 Blend or process roasted nuts, herbs, ginger, garlic, juice, sauce and sugar until smooth. With motor operating, add oil in thin, steady stream; process until pesto thickens.

preparation time 30 minutes
cooking time 1 hour 50 minutes (plus cooling time)
serves 6
nutritional count per serving 30.0g total fat (9.7g saturated fat); 1864kJ (446 cal); 1.6g carbohydrate; 42.2g protein; 1.5g fibre

tip Ask the butcher to bone the lamb shoulder for you.

boned lamb shoulder with coriander hazelnut pesto

slow-roasted lamb shanks with caramelised onion

1 tablespoon olive oil
8 extra-trimmed lamb shanks
(about 1.2kg)
1 tablespoon sugar
1½ cups (375ml) dry red wine
2 cups (500ml) beef stock
3 cloves garlic, crushed
20g butter
1 small onion (80g), chopped
finely
1 trimmed celery stalk (100g),
chopped finely
1 tablespoon plain flour
1 tablespoon tomato paste
4 sprigs fresh rosemary, chopped
coarsely

caramelised onion
40g butter
2 medium red onions (340g),
sliced thinly
¼ cup (50g) brown sugar
¼ cup (60ml) raspberry vinegar

1 Preheat oven to 150°C/130°C fan-assisted.
2 Heat oil in large flameproof baking dish; cook shanks over heat until browned all over. Stir in sugar, wine, stock and garlic; bring to the boil. Roast lamb, covered, in oven, about 4 hours, turning twice during cooking.
3 Meanwhile, make caramelised onion.
4 Remove lamb from dish; cover to keep warm. Pour pan juices into large heatproof jug. Return dish to heat, melt butter; cook onion and celery, stirring, until celery is just tender. Stir in flour; cook, stirring, 2 minutes. Add reserved pan juices, paste and rosemary; bring to the boil. Simmer, uncovered, stirring until it boils and thickens; strain sauce into large jug.
5 Serve lamb with sauce and caramelised onion, accompanied with pureed white beans, if desired.

caramelised onion Melt butter in medium saucepan; cook onion, stirring, about 15 minutes or until browned and soft. Stir in sugar and vinegar; cook, stirring, about 15 minutes or until onion is caramelised.

preparation time 20 minutes
cooking time 4 hours 20 minutes **serves** 4
nutritional count per serving 32.6g total fat (15.9g saturated fat); 2989kJ (715 cal); 27.1g carbohydrate; 61.6g protein; 2.5g fibre

slow-roasted thai lamb shanks

2 star anise
2 teaspoons ground coriander
⅓ cup (100g) tamarind concentrate
2 tablespoons brown sugar
8cm piece fresh ginger (40g), sliced thinly
2 cloves garlic, sliced thinly

1 fresh small red thai chilli, sliced thinly
1 tablespoon kecap manis
1 cup (250ml) water
8 french-trimmed lamb shanks (2kg)
500g choy sum, chopped into 10cm lengths

1 Preheat oven to 180°C/160°C fan-assisted.

2 Dry-fry star anise and coriander in small heated frying pan, stirring, until fragrant. Combine spices with tamarind, sugar, ginger, garlic, chilli, kecap manis and the water in medium jug.

3 Place lamb, in single layer, in large shallow baking dish; drizzle with tamarind mixture. Roast, covered, turning lamb occasionally, 2 hours or until meat is almost falling off the bone. Remove lamb from dish; cover to keep warm.

4 Skim away excess fat from lamb pan juices then strain into small saucepan. Bring sauce to the boil; boil, uncovered, 5 minutes.

5 Steam choy sum until just tender then divide among serving plates. Top with lamb; drizzle with sauce.

preparation time 30 minutes
cooking time 2 hours 15 minutes
serves 4
nutritional count per serving 12.5g total fat (5.6g saturated fat); 1492kJ (357 cal); 11.7g carbohydrate; 48.1g protein; 2.6g fibre

2 teaspoons five-spice powder
1 teaspoon dried chilli flakes
1 cinnamon stick
2 star anise
¼ cup (60ml) soy sauce
½ cup (125ml) chinese
cooking wine
2 tablespoons tamarind
concentrate
2 tablespoons brown sugar
8cm piece fresh ginger (40g),
grated
2 cloves garlic, chopped coarsely
1¼ cups (310ml) water
8 french-trimmed lamb shanks
(1.6kg)
500g choy sum, cut into 10cm
lengths
150g sugar snap peas, trimmed

1 Preheat oven to 180°C/160°C fan-assisted.
2 Dry-fry five-spice, chilli, cinnamon and star anise in small frying pan, stirring, until fragrant. Combine spices with soy sauce, wine, tamarind, sugar, ginger, garlic and the water in medium jug.
3 Place shanks, in single layer, in large shallow baking dish; drizzle with spice mixture. Roast, uncovered, turning shanks occasionally, about 2 hours or until meat is almost falling off the bone. Remove shanks from dish; cover to keep warm. Skim away excess fat from pan juices; strain sauce into small saucepan.
4 Meanwhile, boil, steam or microwave choy sum and peas, separately, until tender; drain.
5 Divide vegetables among serving plates; serve with shanks, drizzled with reheated sauce.

preparation time 20 minutes
cooking time 2 hours 10 minutes
serves 4

nutritional count per serving 20.0g total fat (9.0g saturated fat); 1885kJ (451 cal); 12.5g carbohydrate; 48.3g protein; 3.1g fibre

lamb shanks in five-spice, tamarind & ginger

pork loin with spinach & pancetta stuffing

4 slices white bread (120g)
2 tablespoons olive oil
1 clove garlic, crushed
1 medium onion (150g),
chopped coarsely
6 slices pancetta (90g),
chopped coarsely
100g baby spinach leaves
¼ cup (35g) roasted macadamias,
chopped coarsely
½ cup (125ml) chicken stock
2kg boneless pork loin

plum & red wine sauce
1½ cups (480g) plum jam
2 tablespoons dry red wine
⅔ cup (160ml) chicken stock

1 Preheat oven to 200°C/180°C fan-assisted.
2 Remove and discard bread crusts; cut bread into 1cm cubes. Heat half of the oil in large frying pan; cook bread, stirring, until browned and crisp. Drain croutons on absorbent paper.
3 Heat remaining oil in same pan; cook garlic, onion and pancetta until onion browns lightly. Stir in spinach; remove from heat. Gently stir in croutons, nuts and stock.
4 Place pork on board, fat-side down; slice through thickest part of pork horizontally, without cutting through other side. Open out pork to form one large piece; press stuffing mixture against loin along width of pork. Roll pork to enclose stuffing, securing with kitchen string at 2cm intervals.
5 Place rolled pork on rack in large shallow baking dish. Roast, uncovered, 1¼ hours or until cooked through.
6 Meanwhile, make plum and red wine sauce; serve with sliced pork.

plum & red wine sauce bring ingredients to the boil in small saucepan. Reduce heat; simmer, uncovered, 10 minutes or until sauce thickens slightly.

preparation time 30 minutes
cooking time 1 hour 30 minutes
serves 10
nutritional count per serving 25.7g total fat (7.1g saturated fat); 2458kJ (588 cal); 40.3g carbohydrate; 47.0g protein; 1.8g fibre

pork

roast rolled pork loin & crackling

2.5kg boneless loin of pork, rind on
1 tablespoon olive oil
2 teaspoons fine sea salt
1 tablespoon plain flour
1½ cups (375ml) chicken stock

apricot, prune & rice stuffing
⅔ cup (130g) white long-grain rice
½ cup (75g) finely chopped dried apricots
½ cup (105g) finely chopped prunes

1 Preheat oven to 240°C/220°C fan-assisted.
2 Place pork on board, rind-side up. Run a sharp knife about 5mm under rind, between it and the meat, gradually lifting and easing rind away from pork. Place rind, right-side up, in large shallow flameproof baking dish. Score rind, making diagonal cuts; rub with half of the oil, sprinkle with salt. Roast, uncovered, about 40 minutes or until crackling is well browned and crisp. Chop crackling into serving pieces. Reduce oven temperature to 220°C/200°C fan-assisted.

3 Meanwhile, make apricot, prune and rice stuffing.
4 Place pork, fat-side down, on board. Slice through the thickest part of the meat horizontally, without cutting through at the side. Open out meat to form one large piece; press stuffing against the loin along width. Roll pork to enclose stuffing; secure with kitchen string at 2cm intervals.
5 Return pork to same dish, brush with remaining oil; roast, uncovered, 1 hour or until cooked through. Remove from dish; cover to keep warm.
6 Pour pan juices from pork dish into medium jug. Add 1 tablespoon of the pan juices to pork dish over medium heat, stir in flour; cook, stirring, until mixture bubbles and is browned to your liking. Gradually add remaining pan juices and stock; cook, stirring, until gravy boils and thickens. Pour gravy into serving jug.
7 Serve pork with gravy and reheated crackling.

apricot, prune & rice stuffing cook rice in large saucepan of boiling water, uncovered, 15 minutes or until just tender; drain. Combine cooled rice in large bowl with remaining ingredients.

preparation time 30 minutes
cooking time 2 hours (plus cooling time)
serves 6
nutritional count per serving 96.4g total fat (32.2g saturated fat); 5426kJ (1298 cal); 29.8g carbohydrate; 78.7g protein; 2.7g fibre

2.5kg boneless pork loin with
20cm flap
2 tablespoons coarse cooking salt
3 cups (750ml) sparkling cider
½ cup (125ml) chicken stock
3 teaspoons white sugar

apple stuffing
30g butter
3 large granny smith apples
(600g), peeled, cored, cut into
thin wedges
1 medium leek (350g), sliced
thinly
1 medium onion (150g), sliced
thinly
½ teaspoon ground cinnamon
2 tablespoons white sugar
1 cup (70g) stale breadcrumbs
1 tablespoon finely grated
lemon rind
1 cup coarsely chopped fresh
flat-leaf parsley

1 Preheat oven to 240°C/220°C
fan-assisted.
2 Place pork on board, rind-side
up. Run sharp knife about 5mm
under rind, gradually lifting rind
away; place rind in large shallow
baking dish. Using sharp knife,
score rind at 3cm intervals forming
diamonds; rub with salt. Roast,
uncovered, 30 minutes or until
crackling is browned and crisp.
Chop crackling into serving
pieces; reserve.
3 Reduce oven temperature to
180°C/160°C fan-assisted.
4 Meanwhile, make apple stuffing.
5 Slice through the thickest part
of pork horizontally, without cutting
all the way through. Open pork out
to form one large piece; press
stuffing against the loin along
length of pork. Roll pork to enclose
stuffing; secure with kitchen string
at 2cm intervals.

6 Place pork on wire rack in large
shallow flameproof baking dish;
pour 2½ cups of the cider into
dish. Roast, uncovered, about
1½ hours or until cooked through.
Remove pork from baking dish;
cover to keep warm.
7 Place baking dish over heat,
add stock, sugar and remaining
cider; cook, stirring, until sauce
thickens slightly.
8 Serve pork and crackling with
sauce and, if desired, braised red
cabbage.

apple stuffing heat butter in
large frying pan; cook apple, leek,
onion, cinnamon and sugar, stirring,
until leek and onion soften.
Remove from heat; stir in
breadcrumbs, rind and parsley.

preparation time 1 hour
cooking time 2 hours
15 minutes
serves 8
nutritional count per serving
23.9g total fat (9.2g saturated
fat); 2387kJ (571 cal); 27.6g
carbohydrate; 59.6g protein;
2.9g fibre

apple-stuffed pork loin

1 cup (70g) stale multigrain breadcrumbs
3 cloves garlic, crushed
1 tablespoon coarsely chopped fresh sage
¼ cup (40g) pitted prunes, chopped coarsely
¼ cup (45g) finely chopped dried figs
2 tablespoons greek-style yogurt
1.7kg lean pork loin
1 tablespoon lemon juice
1 tablespoon coarse cooking salt
2 medium onions (300g), cut into wedges
3 small firm pears (440g), quartered
1kg salad potatoes, halved lengthways
2 tablespoons olive oil

1 Preheat the oven to 240°C/220°C fan-assisted.

2 Combine breadcrumbs, garlic, sage, prunes, figs and yogurt in small bowl. Place mixture against the pork loin along the length. Roll pork to enclose seasoning; secure with kitchen string at 2cm intervals.

3 Place pork on oiled wire rack in medium baking dish; rub with combined juice and salt. Roast, uncovered, about 20 minutes or until skin blisters. Drain fat from dish. Reduce oven temperature to 180°C/160°C fan-assisted; add onion and pear to dish, roast, uncovered, 20 minutes.

4 Place combined potatoes and oil in separate medium baking dish; roast, uncovered, 50 minutes or until pork is cooked through and potatoes are tender.

5 Serve pork with onion, pears and potatoes.

preparation time 40 minutes
cooking time 1 hour 10 minutes
serves 6
nutritional count per serving 70.6g total fat (22.8g saturated fat); 4452kJ (1065 cal); 46.3g carbohydrate; 58.7g protein; 8.1g fibre

pork loin with prunes, potatoes & pears

honey-glazed pork with sage

2.5kg boneless loin of pork
2 teaspoons vegetable oil
1 tablespoon fine sea salt
2 cloves garlic, crushed
1 tablespoon finely chopped fresh sage
⅓ cup (90g) honey, warmed
1 tablespoon red wine vinegar
2 cups (500ml) chicken stock
2 tablespoons cornflour
2 tablespoons water

1 Preheat oven to 240°C/220°C fan-assisted.
2 Place pork rind, fat-side down, on oiled wire rack in large flameproof baking dish; rub oil and salt into it. Roast, uncovered, about 30 minutes or until crackling is crisp and browned; cool. Discard fat from baking dish.
3 Place pork, fat-side down, on board; sprinkle with half of the garlic and half of the sage. Roll pork to enclose sage and garlic; secure with kitchen string at 2cm intervals. Place pork on wire rack in same baking dish.
4 Reduce oven temperature to 200°C/180°C fan-assisted; roast pork, uncovered, 30 minutes. Cover with foil; reduce oven temperature to 180°C/160°C fan-assisted. Roast 1 hour.
5 Combine honey, vinegar and remaining sage and garlic in small bowl. Remove foil from pork, brush pork with half of the honey mixture.

Roast, uncovered, 30 minutes or until browned and cooked through, brushing occasionally with remaining honey mixture. Remove pork from dish; cover with foil.
6 Strain pan juices from baking dish into heatproof jug; remove fat from pan juices (you will need ⅔ cup of pan juices). Add stock to baking dish; stir in combined cornflour and water over heat until sauce boils and thickens. Serve pork slices with sauce and crackling.

preparation time 20 minutes
cooking time 2 hours 45 minutes
serves 8
nutritional count per serving 71.1g total fat (24.0g saturated fat); 3804kJ (910 cal); 12.0g carbohydrate; 57.3g protein; 0.1g fibre

tip Ask your butcher to remove the rind completely from the pork loin and score it.

leg of pork with apple & onion compote

4kg leg of pork
2 tablespoons fresh sage leaves
2 cloves garlic, sliced thinly
1 tablespoon olive oil
2 tablespoons salt
1 teaspoon fennel seeds

apple & onion compote
40g butter
3 large onions (600g), sliced thinly
2 tablespoons sugar
¼ cup (60ml) cider vinegar
¾ cup (180ml) water
4 large apples (180g), peeled, sliced

1 Preheat oven to 240°C/220°C fan-assisted.
2 Using sharp knife, pierce pork about 12 times all over, gently twisting to make a small hole. Press sage and sliced garlic evenly into holes.
3 Rub rind with oil and salt, rub underside of the pork with fennel seeds. Place pork on oiled wire rack in baking dish. Roast, uncovered, 30 minutes or until rind blisters. Reduce oven temperature to 180°C/160°C fan-assisted; roast further 2½ hours or until cooked through.

4 Meanwhile, make apple and onion compote.
5 Serve pork with compote and steamed green beans, if desired.

apple & onion compote
heat butter in large frying pan; cook onion, stirring occasionally, about 10 minutes. Add sugar; cook, stirring occasionally about 10 minutes or until onion caramelises. Stir in vinegar, water and apples; bring to the boil. Reduce heat; simmer, covered about 15 minutes or until apples are soft.

preparation time 30 minutes
cooking time 3 hours
serves 10
nutritional count per serving 28.6g total fat (10.4g saturated fat); 2437kJ (583 cal); 14.6g carbohydrate; 65.6g protein; 2.1g fibre

2 tablespoons finely grated
lemon rind
3 cloves garlic, crushed
1 teaspoon cracked black pepper
1 tablespoon olive oil
2.6kg full rack of pork
6 fresh bay leaves
1 tablespoon olive oil, extra
2 teaspoons cooking salt
½ cup (125ml) dry white wine
2½ cups (625ml) chicken stock
2 teaspoons cornflour
1 tablespoon water

1 Preheat oven to 240°C/220°C fan-assisted.
2 Combine lemon rind, garlic, pepper and oil in small bowl; rub underside of rack. Place bay leaves on oiled wire rack in large shallow flameproof baking dish; top with pork.
3 Rub pork rind with extra oil; sprinkle with salt. Roast, uncovered, about 30 minutes or until rind blisters. Reduce oven temperature to 180°C/160°C fan-assisted; roast further 1 hour 15 minutes or until pork is just cooked through.

Remove pork from dish; cover to keep warm.
4 Drain excess fat from baking dish. Place dish over heat, add wine; cook, stirring, until wine is reduced by half. Add stock; bring to the boil. Stir in blended cornflour and water; cook, stirring, until mixture boils and thickens. Strain into serving jug.
5 Serve pork with sauce.

preparation time 20 minutes
cooking time 2 hours
serves 10
nutritional count per serving
50.0g total fat (16.4g saturated fat); 2353kJ (563 cal); 1.1g carbohydrate; 26.8g protein; 0.2g fibre

tip Ask your butcher to score the rind of the pork diagonally.

lemon and garlic rack of pork

crackling pork with apple & cider sauce

8-rib rack of pork (2kg)
1 tablespoon coarse cooking salt
9 baby onions (225g), halved
3 trimmed celery stalks (300g),
cut into 8cm lengths
⅔ cup loosely packed fresh
flat-leaf parsley leaves

apple & cider sauce
10g butter
2 shallots (50g), sliced thinly
2 medium green apples (300g),
peeled, cored, sliced thinly
¾ cup (180ml) dry cider
1 tablespoon white sugar
2 teaspoons lemon juice
¼ teaspoon salt

1 Preheat oven to 240°C/220°C fan-assisted. Place pork in large baking dish; rub scored rind with salt. Roast pork, uncovered, 25 minutes or until rind blisters. Drain excess fat from dish.
2 Reduce oven temperature to 180°C/160°C fan-assisted. Add onions and celery to baking dish with pork. Roast pork and vegetables for a further 45 minutes or until cooked through. Turn or shake vegetables occasionally during cooking.
3 Meanwhile, make apple and cider sauce.
4 Remove pork and vegetables from oven. Cover with foil; stand pork 10 minutes before slicing. Remove vegetables from dish, toss with parsley.
5 Serve pork with sauce and vegetable mixture.

apple & cider sauce heat butter in medium saucepan; cook shallots, stirring, until softened. Add apple; cook, stirring, 2 minutes. Add cider; bring to the boil. Boil, uncovered, 1 minute. Cover, simmer, 5 to 10 minutes or until apples are tender and cider has reduced slightly. Stir in sugar, juice and salt. Blend or process apple mixture until smooth.

preparation time 20 minutes
cooking time 1 hour 30 minutes
serves 8
nutritional count per serving 36.3g total fat (12.6g saturated fat); 2011kJ (481 cal); 7.9g carbohydrate; 29.3g protein; 1.7g fibre

tips Ask your butcher to score the rind, 1cm apart, across the pork in the same direction as you will slice. The rind should be scored deeply, through to the fat, to ensure the fat is rendered and the crackling will be crisp. This recipe is best made close to serving.

roast pork with garlic & rosemary

1.5kg neck of pork
3 cloves garlic, crushed
1 tablespoon chopped fresh rosemary
1 tablespoon coarse cooking salt
2 tablespoons olive oil
3 bay leaves
1 cup (250ml) water
⅓ cup (80ml) red wine vinegar

1 Preheat oven to 200°C/180°C fan-assisted.
2 Tie pork with kitchen string at 3cm intervals.
3 Combine garlic, rosemary, salt and oil in small bowl; rub mixture over pork. Place pork on wire rack in baking dish; add bay leaves, the water and vinegar to dish.
4 Roast pork about 1½ hours or until cooked through. Cover pork; stand 10 minutes before slicing.

preparation time 20 minutes
cooking time 1 hour 30 minutes (plus standing time)
serves 6
nutritional count per serving 26.1g total fat (7.6g saturated fat); 1877kJ (449 cal); 0.2g carbohydrate; 53.1g protein; 0.3g fibre

1.5kg neck of pork
1 clove garlic, crushed
1 teaspoon fennel seeds
1 tablespoon olive oil
⅔ cup (160ml) dry white wine
⅓ cup (80ml) chicken stock
6 medium fennel bulbs (1.8kg),
halved lengthways
80g butter, softened
3 cloves garlic, sliced thinly

1 Tie pork with kitchen string at 2cm intervals. Combine crushed garlic and seeds; rub over pork.
2 Preheat oven to 150°C/130°C fan-assisted.
3 Heat oil in large flameproof baking dish; cook pork, uncovered, over heat until browned all over. Add wine and stock; bring to the boil. Cover dish tightly with foil; roast, covered, in oven 1½ hours.
4 Add fennel to dish, dot with combined butter and garlic; roast, covered, further 1¼ hours, turning pork and fennel occasionally.

5 Increase oven temperature to 220°C/200°C fan-assisted. Remove foil from pork, spoon pan juices over pork and fennel; roast, uncovered, about 20 minutes or until browned. Transfer pork and fennel to serving platter, cover; stand 15 minutes.
6 Meanwhile, place baking dish over heat; bring pan juices to the boil. Reduce heat; simmer, uncovered, until mixture reduces to about 2 cups.

7 Serve pork and fennel drizzled with pan juices.

preparation time 25 minutes
cooking time 3 hours
25 minutes (plus standing time)
serves 6
nutritional count per serving 34.2g total fat (14.4g saturated fat); 2412kJ (577 cal); 5.9g carbohydrate; 55.1g protein; 5.1g fibre

slow-roasted pork with fennel

barbecue spareribs

Ask your butcher to cut pork spareribs 'American-style' for this recipe. Trimmed of almost all fat, the meat usually comes in racks of 8 to 10 ribs.

3.5kg american-style pork spareribs

barbecue sauce
2¼ cups (560ml) tomato sauce
1½ cups (375ml) cider vinegar
⅓ cup (80ml) olive oil
½ cup (125ml) worcestershire sauce
¾ cup (165g) firmly packed brown sugar
⅓ cup (95g) american-style mustard
1½ teaspoons cracked black pepper
3 fresh small red thai chillies, chopped finely
3 cloves garlic, crushed
¼ cup (60ml) lemon juice

1 Make barbecue sauce.
2 Brush both sides of ribs with barbecue sauce; place in large deep baking dish. Pour remaining sauce over ribs, cover; refrigerate overnight, turning ribs occasionally in the sauce.
3 Preheat oven to 160°C/140°C fan-assisted.
4 Drain ribs; reserve sauce. Divide ribs between two wire racks over two large shallow baking dishes. Roast, covered, 1½ hours; brush with sauce every 20 minutes. Turn ribs midway through cooking time.

5 Increase oven temperature to 220°C/200°C fan-assisted. Uncover ribs; roast, brushing frequently with sauce, until ribs are browned and cooked through, turning after 15 minutes.
6 Place remaining barbecue sauce in small saucepan; bring to the boil. Reduce heat; simmer, stirring, about 4 minutes or until sauce thickens slightly. Using scissors, cut ribs in portions of two or three ribs; serve ribs with hot sauce.

barbecue sauce bring ingredients to the boil in medium saucepan. Remove from heat; cool.

preparation time 25 minutes (plus refrigeration time)
cooking time 2 hours 10 minutes
serves 8
nutritional count per serving 12.9g total fat (2.3g saturated fat); 1998kJ (478 cal); 42.1g carbohydrate; 46.5g protein; 2.2g fibre

Ask your butcher to slice
spareribs thinly, about
2cm thick. Recipe can be
prepared two days ahead;
reheat ribs in a hot oven
before serving.

1kg pork belly spareribs
¾ cup (180ml) char siu sauce
½ cup (125ml) chicken stock
1 clove garlic, crushed

1 Cut ribs into serving-sized
pieces; remove rind if desired.
2 Combine rib pieces in large
bowl with remaining ingredients.
Cover; refrigerate 3 hours or
overnight, stirring mixture
occasionally.
3 Preheat oven to 200°C/180°C
fan-assisted.
4 Line base and sides of large
baking dish with foil or pour
enough boiling water into dish to
just cover base. Place ribs on oiled
wire rack in dish; reserve marinade.
Roast, uncovered, 25 minutes or
until ribs are tender and browned,
brushing twice with reserved
marinade during cooking.

preparation time 10 minutes
(plus refrigeration time)
cooking time 25 minutes
makes about 36 pieces
nutritional count per piece
6.5g total fat (2.2g saturated fat);
368kJ (88 cal); 2.0g carbohydrate;
5.2g protein; 0.6g fibre

roasted char siu pork spareribs

chinese barbecued spareribs

¾ cup (180ml) barbecue sauce
2 tablespoons dark soy sauce
1 tablespoon honey
¼ cup (60ml) orange juice
2 tablespoons brown sugar
1 clove garlic, crushed
2cm piece fresh ginger (10g), grated
2kg american-style pork spareribs (see page 76)

1 Combine sauces, honey, juice, sugar, garlic and ginger in large shallow dish; add ribs, turn to coat in marinade. Cover; refrigerate 3 hours or overnight.
2 Preheat oven to 180°C/160°C fan-assisted.
3 Brush ribs both sides with marinade; place, in single layer, in large shallow baking dish; roast, covered, 45 minutes. Uncover; roast about 15 minutes or until ribs are browned. Serve with fried rice, if desired.

preparation time 15 minutes (plus refrigeration time)
cooking time 1 hour
serves 4
nutritional count per serving 26.4g total fat (10.2g saturated fat); 2675kJ (640 cal); 35.2g carbohydrate; 64.7g protein; 0.8g fibre

honey sesame ribs

4 racks american-style pork spareribs (1.5kg) (see page 76)

honey sesame marinade
¼ cup (90g) honey
½ cup (125ml) kecap manis
2 teaspoons sesame oil
2 star anise
1 tablespoon sesame seeds, toasted
10g piece fresh ginger, grated
1 clove garlic, crushed

1 Combine ingredients for honey sesame marinade in small bowl.
2 Place pork in large shallow dish; add two-thirds of the marinade. Cover; refrigerate 3 hours or overnight, turning occasionally.
3 Preheat oven to 160°C/140°C fan-assisted. Line two baking dishes with baking paper or foil; place oiled wire rack in each dish.
4 Drain pork. Place pork, in single layer, on racks in dishes. Roast, uncovered, 45 minutes, turning halfway and brushing with remaining marinade until well browned and cooked through.

preparation time 20 minutes (plus refrigeration time)
cooking time 45 minutes
serves 6

nutritional count per serving 11.6g total fat (3.4g saturated fat); 1083kJ (259 cal); 13.0g carbohydrate; 25.5g protein; 0.3g fibre

1.5kg large pork fillets
2 cloves garlic, sliced thinly lengthways
16 small fresh sage leaves
1 teaspoon fennel seeds
2 tablespoons olive oil
1 medium onion (150g), sliced
¾ cup (180ml) chicken stock
¼ cup (60ml) fresh orange juice

1 Cut a few small slits along the top of pork; push in garlic and sage. Sprinkle pork with seeds; stand 30 minutes.

2 Preheat oven to 220°C/200°C fan-assisted.

3 Heat half of the oil in large flameproof baking dish; cook pork over heat until browned all over. Remove from dish.

4 Heat remaining oil in same dish; cook onion, stirring, until lightly browned. Return pork to dish; drizzle with stock and juice. Roast, uncovered, in oven 10 minutes or until pork is cooked through. Cover pork; stand 10 minutes.

5 Serve sliced pork with seasoned pan juices and mixed salad leaves, if desired.

preparation time 10 minutes
cooking time 35 minutes
(plus standing time)
serves 8
nutritional count per serving
19.7g total fat (5.8g saturated fat); 1446kJ (346 cal); 1.9g carbohydrate; 40.4g protein; 0.4g fibre

roasted pork fillets with orange

pork fillets with apple and leek

800g pork fillets
¾ cup (180ml) chicken stock
2 medium leeks (700g),
sliced thickly
1 clove garlic, crushed
2 tablespoons brown sugar
2 tablespoons red wine vinegar
2 medium apples (300g)
10g butter
1 tablespoon brown sugar, extra
400g baby carrots, trimmed,
halved
8 medium patty-pan squash
(100g), quartered
250g asparagus, trimmed,
chopped coarsely

1 Preheat oven to 240°C/220°C fan-assisted.
2 Place pork, in single layer, in large baking dish; roast, uncovered, about 25 minutes or until pork is browned and cooked through. Cover; stand 5 minutes before slicing thickly.
3 Meanwhile, heat half of the stock in medium frying pan; cook leek and garlic, stirring, until leek softens and browns slightly. Add sugar and vinegar; cook, stirring, about 5 minutes or until leek caramelises. Add remaining stock; bring to the boil.

Reduce heat; simmer, uncovered, about 5 minutes or until liquid reduces by half. Place leek mixture in medium bowl; cover to keep warm.
4 Peel, core and halve apples; cut into thick slices. Melt butter in same pan; cook apple and extra sugar, stirring, until apple is browned and tender.
5 Boil, steam or microwave carrot, squash and asparagus, separately, until just tender; drain.
6 Divide mixed vegetables among serving plates, top with pork, sweet and sour leek, then apple.

preparation time 10 minutes
cooking time 25 minutes
serves 4
nutritional count per serving
6.1g total fat (2.4g saturated fat);
1605kJ (384 cal); 26.5g
carbohydrate; 51.0g protein;
8.3g fibre

tip sweet and sour leek can be made several hours ahead; just reheat before serving.

roasted pork belly with plum sauce

800g boneless pork belly, rind on
2 teaspoons fine sea salt
1 teaspoon olive oil
1 cup (250ml) water
1½ cups (375ml) chicken stock
2 tablespoons soy sauce
¼ cup (60ml) chinese cooking wine
¼ cup (55g) firmly packed brown sugar
2 cloves garlic, sliced thinly
3cm piece fresh ginger (15g), sliced thinly
1 cinnamon stick, crushed
1 teaspoon dried chilli flakes
⅓ cup (80ml) orange juice
6 whole cloves
1 teaspoon fennel seeds
4 plums (450g), cut into eight wedges

cucumber salad
½ cucumber (130g)
1 fresh long green chilli, sliced thinly
⅔ cup coarsely chopped fresh mint
1 tablespoon olive oil
1 tablespoon lemon juice
1 teaspoon caster sugar

1 Preheat oven to 180°C/160°C fan-assisted. Place pork on board, rind-side up. Using sharp knife, score rind by making shallow cuts diagonally in both directions at 3cm intervals; rub combined salt and oil into cuts.

2 Combine the water, stock, soy sauce, wine, sugar, garlic, ginger, cinnamon, chilli, juice, cloves and seeds in large shallow baking dish. Place pork in dish, rind-side up; roast, uncovered, 1 hour 20 minutes. Increase oven temperature to 240°C/220°C fan-assisted. Roast pork, uncovered, further 15 minutes or until crackling is crisp. Remove from dish; cover to keep warm.

3 Strain pan juices from dish into saucepan, skim away surface fat; bring to the boil. Add plums; simmer, uncovered, 15 minutes or until thickened.

4 Meanwhile, make cucumber salad; serve with sliced pork and sauce.

cucumber salad using vegetable peeler, cut cucumber lengthways into ribbons. Place in large bowl with remaining ingredients; toss to combine.

preparation time 20 minutes
cooking time 1 hour 55 minutes
serves 4
nutritional count per serving 51.0g total fat (16.2g saturated fat); 3010kJ (720 cal); 25.6g carbohydrate; 39.1g protein; 3.4g fibre

1kg boneless pork belly, skin on
½ cup (125ml) chinese cooking wine
¼ cup (60ml) soy sauce
1 tablespoon tamarind concentrate
2 tablespoons honey
½ teaspoon sesame oil
4cm piece fresh ginger (20g), chopped finely
3 cloves garlic, crushed
2 teaspoons five-spice powder
1 star anise
1 dried long red chilli
1 teaspoon sichuan pepper
3 cups (750ml) water
900g baby pak choi, halved lengthways

1 Place pork in large saucepan of boiling water; return to the boil. Reduce heat; simmer, uncovered, about 40 minutes or until pork is cooked through, drain.
2 Combine pork in large bowl with wine, soy sauce, tamarind, honey, oil, ginger, garlic, five-spice, star anise, chilli, pepper and the water. Cover; refrigerate 3 hours or overnight.
3 Preheat oven to 220°C/200°C fan-assisted.

4 Place pork, skin-side up, on oiled wire rack in large shallow baking dish; reserve marinade. Pour enough water into baking dish to come halfway up side of dish. Roast pork, uncovered, 30 minutes or until browned.
5 Meanwhile, strain marinade into small saucepan; bring to the boil. Boil, uncovered, 20 minutes or until reduced to about 1 cup. Boil, steam or microwave pak choi until just tender; drain.
6 Serve pork with sauce and pak choi.

preparation time 10 minutes (plus refrigeration time)
cooking time 1 hour 25 minutes
serves 6
nutritional count per serving 37.9g total fat (12.7g saturated fat); 2195kJ (525 cal); 10.3g carbohydrate; 32.6g protein; 2.4g fibre

asian-spiced roasted pork belly

baked ham with redcurrant glaze

¾ cup (290g) redcurrant jelly
2 tablespoons balsamic vinegar
¼ cup (50g) firmly packed
brown sugar
3 cloves
8kg leg of ham
1 cup (250ml) water
20 baby onions (600g)

1 Preheat oven to 180°C/160°C
fan-assisted.
2 Stir jelly, vinegar, sugar and
cloves in medium saucepan over
medium heat until sugar is
dissolved. Reserve ¼ cup glaze for
the onions.

3 Cut through rind about 10cm
from shank end of leg in decorative
pattern; run thumb around edge of
rind just under skin to remove rind.
Start pulling rind from widest edge
of ham, continue to pull carefully
away from fat up to decorative
pattern; discard rind.
4 Using sharp knife, score fat by
making shallow cuts diagonally in
both directions at 3cm intervals.
5 Place ham on oiled wire rack in
a large baking dish; pour in the
water. Brush ham all over with
glaze. Cover shank end with foil;
roast, uncovered, 45 minutes.

6 Meanwhile, add onions to small
baking dish with reserved glaze
and 2 tablespoons water. Cover
with foil; roast with ham for further
45 minutes or until tender. Brush
ham with glaze every 30 minutes.
7 Serve ham with onions.

preparation time 30 minutes
cooking time 1 hour 30 minutes
serves 10
nutritional count per serving
33.8g total fat (12.4g saturated
fat); 3566kJ (853 cal); 26.8g
carbohydrate; 109.1g protein;
1.1g fibre

honey ginger-glazed ham

8kg cooked leg of ham
2 teaspoons cloves
⅔ cup (230g) honey
½ cup (115g) stem ginger,
chopped coarsely
½ cup (100g) firmly packed
brown sugar
2¼ cups (560ml) water

1 Preheat oven to 180°C/160°C
fan-assisted.
2 Prepare ham as in steps 3 and
4 of recipe above. Push a clove in
centre of each diamond shape.
3 Stir honey, ginger, sugar and
¼ cup (60ml) of the water in small
saucepan over low heat until sugar
dissolves. Blend or process mixture
until smooth.
4 Pour remaining water into large
baking dish; place ham on oiled
wire rack over dish. Brush ham
with glaze; cover shank end with
foil. Roast, uncovered, about
1 hour or until browned all over,
brushing frequently with glaze.

preparation time 30 minutes
cooking time 1 hour 5 minutes
serves 10

nutritional count per serving
33.8g total fat (12.4g saturated
fat); 3733kJ (893 cal); 38.0g
carbohydrate; 108.4g protein;
0.1g fibre

salmon with herb & walnut crust

1kg piece salmon fillet
1 tablespoon extra virgin olive oil
½ cup coarsely chopped fresh flat-leaf parsley
¼ cup coarsely chopped fresh dill
1 clove garlic, crushed
2 teaspoons finely grated lemon rind
¼ cup (30g) coarsely chopped roasted walnuts
2 teaspoons lemon juice
1 tablespoon extra virgin olive oil, extra

1 Preheat oven to 200°C/180°C fan-assisted.
2 Place salmon in large baking dish; brush with oil. Roast for 5 minutes.
3 Meanwhile, combine remaining ingredients in medium bowl.
4 Remove salmon from oven, sprinkle with three-quarters of the parsley mixture. Roast salmon further 5 minutes. The salmon will be rare in the thicker end of the fillet – you can adjust cooking time to suit your taste.
5 Transfer salmon to serving platter; sprinkle with remaining parsley mixture. Serve with lemon wedges, if desired.

preparation time 10 minutes
cooking time 10 minutes
serves 6
nutritional count per serving 21.4g total fat (3.7g saturated fat); 1367kJ (327 cal); 0.3g carbohydrate; 33.4g protein; 0.7g fibre

tip herb and walnut mixture can be made several hours ahead. The salmon can be cooked several hours ahead and served cold, if preferred; otherwise, roast close to serving.

fish

slow-roasted salmon with spring onions & peas

300g spring onions
2 medium brown onions (300g)
60g butter
2 cloves garlic, sliced thinly
½ cup (125ml) vegetable stock
1kg fresh peas, shelled (or 350g shelled peas)
1 medium lemon (150g)
1kg side salmon
1 teaspoon cracked black pepper
1 teaspoon sea salt

1 Preheat oven to 120°C/100°C fan-assisted.

2 Trim roots and half of the tops from spring onions. Cut brown onions into wedges.

3 Heat butter in large baking dish; cook brown onion and garlic, stirring gently, until browned lightly. Add stock and peas; roast, uncovered, about 30 minutes or until onions are soft.

4 Meanwhile, remove rind from lemon with a zester (or peel rind thinly from lemon, avoiding white pith then cut rind into thin strips); squeeze 2 tablespoons juice from lemon.

5 Add spring onions to baking dish; place salmon on top of onion mixture. Sprinkle salmon with rind, juice, pepper and salt. Roast, uncovered, about 20 minutes or until salmon is cooked as desired.

6 Serve salmon and vegetable mixture with pan juices.

preparation time 20 minutes
cooking time 1 hour
serves 6
nutritional count per serving 20.6g total fat (8.1g saturated fat); 1639kJ (392 cal); 11.4g carbohydrate; 37.9g protein; 5.6g fibre

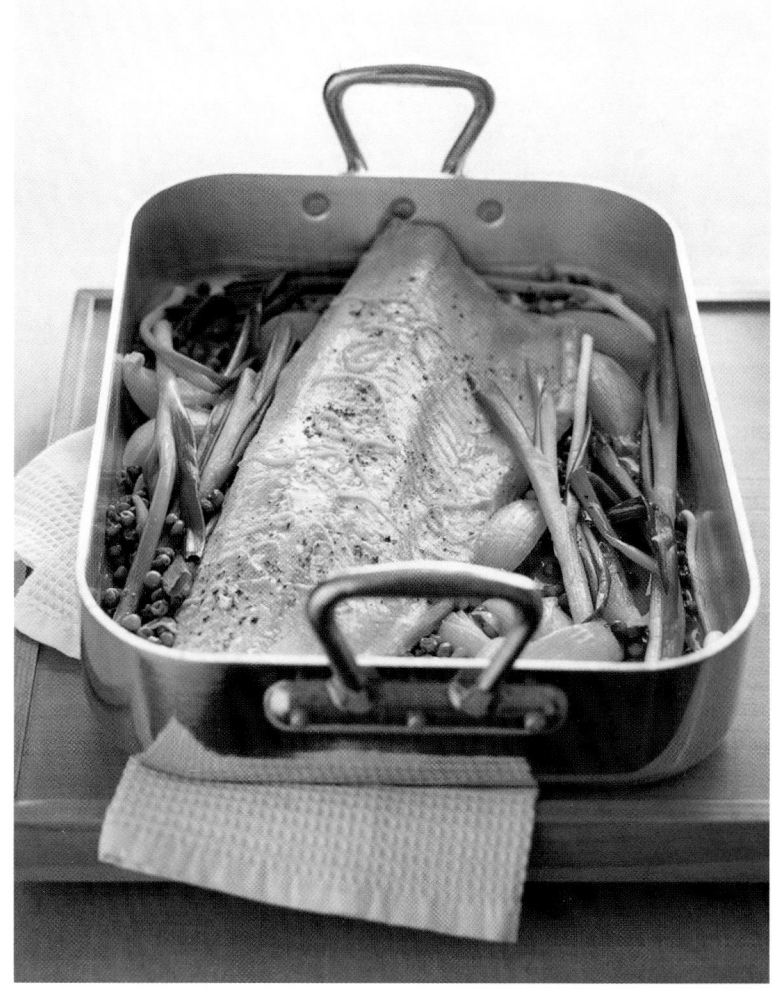

4 x 200g salmon fillets
¼ cup (70g) tandoori curry paste
2 tablespoons natural yogurt
2 teaspoons lemon juice
2 tablespoons groundnut oil
1 large white onion (200g), sliced
2 cloves garlic, sliced
½ teaspoon cumin seeds
½ teaspoon coriander seeds
pinch ground turmeric
1½ cups (300g) basmati rice
3½ cups (875ml) chicken stock
2 teaspoons grated lemon rind

cucumber & mint raita
½ medium cucumber (75g)
1 tablespoon chopped fresh mint
¾ cup (200g) natural yogurt

1 Place salmon in non-metallic dish; pour combined paste, yogurt and juice over fish. (If time permits, cover and refrigerate 2 hours.)
2 Meanwhile, preheat oven to 200°C/180°C fan-assisted.
3 Heat oil in flameproof baking dish; cook onion, garlic and spices, stirring over heat, until onion softens. Add rice; stir until coated with oil. Stir in stock and rind; bring to the boil. Remove from heat, cover tightly with lid or foil; roast in oven 15 minutes.
4 Uncover rice, top with salmon; roast further 8 minutes or until salmon is cooked as desired.
5 Meanwhile, make cucumber and mint raita.

6 Serve salmon with rice and raita; sprinkle with coriander, if desired.

cucumber & mint raita halve cucumber lengthways; remove and discard seeds. Chop cucumber finely; combine with mint and yogurt in small bowl.

preparation time 20 minutes (plus refrigeration time)
cooking time 35 minutes
serves 4
nutritional count per serving 32.2g total fat (7.3g saturated fat); 3244kJ (776 cal); 68.4g carbohydrate; 51.1g protein; 3.6g fibre

tandoori salmon with pilaf & raita

slow-roasted pesto salmon

1 cup loosely packed fresh
basil leaves
2 cloves garlic, chopped coarsely
2 tablespoons roasted pine nuts
2 tablespoons lemon juice
¼ cup (60ml) olive oil
1.5kg piece salmon fillet, skin on
2 tablespoons olive oil, extra
2 large red peppers (700g),
chopped coarsely
1 large red onion (300g),
chopped coarsely

1 Preheat oven to 160°C/140°C fan-assisted.
2 Blend or process basil, garlic, nuts and juice until combined. With motor operating, gradually add oil in thin, steady stream until pesto thickens slightly.
3 Place fish, skin-side down, on piece of oiled foil large enough to completely enclose fish; coat fish with half the pesto. Gather corners of foil together above fish; twist to enclose securely. Place parcel on oven tray; roast about 45 minutes or until cooked as desired.

4 Meanwhile, heat extra oil in large frying pan; cook pepper and onion, stirring, until onion softens.
5 Serve salmon topped with onion mixture and drizzled with remaining pesto.

preparation time 20 minutes
cooking time 45 minutes
serves 8
nutritional count per serving 27.5g total fat (4.8g saturated fat); 1802kJ (431 cal); 6.1g carbohydrate; 39.2g protein; 2.0g fibre

baked fish with ginger and soy

800g whole white fish
4cm piece ginger (20g), grated
1 tablespoon groundnut oil
¼ cup (60ml) chinese cooking wine
¼ cup (60ml) soy sauce
½ teaspoon white sugar
3 spring onions, sliced thinly

1 Preheat oven to 200°C/180°C fan-assisted.
2 Cut three deep slits in each side of fish; place in oiled baking dish.
3 Rub ginger into fish; drizzle with combined oil, wine, sauce and sugar. Bake fish, covered, about 25 minutes or until cooked through.
4 Serve fish drizzled with some of the pan juices, topped with onion.

preparation time 10 minutes
cooking time 25 minutes
serves 2
nutritional count per serving 11.6g total fat (2.6g saturated fat); 1120kJ (268 cal); 3.7g carbohydrate; 32.9g protein; 0.5g fibre

3 Meanwhile, dip vine leaves in medium saucepan of boiling water for 10 seconds; transfer immediately to medium bowl of iced water. Drain on absorbent paper. Slightly overlap two vine leaves, vein-sides up, on board; centre one fish fillet on leaves, top with a quarter of the rind and a quarter of the reserved frond tips. Fold leaves over to enclose fish. Repeat with remaining leaves, fish, rind and frond tips. Place vine-leaf parcels on oiled oven tray; bake about 15 minutes or until fish is cooked as desired.

4 Stir grapes into hot fennel mixture; stand, covered, 2 minutes before serving with fish.

preparation time 20 minutes
cooking time 50 minutes
serves 4
nutritional count per serving 12.5g total fat (2.5g saturated fat); 1433kJ (342 cal); 13.6g carbohydrate; 41.0g protein; 3.8g fibre

tip you can purchase vacuum-packed vine leaves from Middle-Eastern food and Greek or Cypriot delicatessens; rinse and dry well before using.

2 medium fennel bulbs (600g), untrimmed
1 large onion (200g), sliced thinly
2 cloves garlic, sliced thinly
1 tablespoon olive oil
¼ cup (60ml) orange juice
½ cup (125ml) chicken stock
¼ cup (60ml) dry white wine
8 large fresh vine leaves
4 x 200g ocean trout fillets
1 tablespoon finely grated orange rind
180g seedless white grapes

1 Preheat oven to 180°C/160°C fan-assisted.

2 Reserve enough frond tips to make ¼ cup before trimming fennel bulbs. Slice fennel thinly then combine in large shallow baking dish with onion, garlic, oil, juice, stock and wine. Bake, covered, in oven 30 minutes. Uncover, stir; bake, uncovered, further 20 minutes or until vegetables soften, stirring occasionally.

vineleaf-wrapped ocean trout with braised fennel

salt-baked whole ocean trout in saffron cream sauce

3kg cooking salt
4 egg whites
2.4kg whole ocean trout
1.5kg baby new potatoes
3 whole unpeeled bulbs garlic, halved horizontally
¼ cup (60ml) olive oil
15 sprigs fresh thyme
350g watercress, trimmed

saffron cream sauce
¾ cup (180ml) dry white wine
¼ cup (60ml) white wine vinegar
1 tablespoon lemon juice
pinch saffron threads
½ cup (125ml) double cream
170g butter, chilled, chopped finely

1 Preheat oven to 200°C/180°C fan-assisted.
2 Mix salt with egg whites in medium bowl. Spread about half of the salt mixture evenly over base of large baking dish; place fish on salt mixture, cover completely (except for tail) with remaining salt mixture. Bake 1 hour.
3 Meanwhile, combine potatoes, garlic, oil and thyme in large shallow baking dish; place in oven on shelf below fish. Bake, uncovered, about 50 minutes or until potatoes are tender.
4 Make saffron cream sauce.
5 Remove fish from oven; break salt crust with heavy knife, taking care not to cut into fish. Discard salt crust; transfer fish to large serving plate. Carefully remove skin from fish; flake meat into large pieces.

6 Divide watercress, potatoes and garlic among serving plates; top with fish, drizzle with sauce.

saffron cream sauce bring wine, vinegar, juice and saffron in medium saucepan to the boil. Boil until mixture is reduced to about a third. Add cream; return to the boil, then whisk in butter, one piece at a time, until mixture thickens slightly. Pour into medium jug; cover to keep warm.

preparation time 30 minutes
cooking time 1 hour 10 minutes
serves 6
nutritional count per serving 50.4g total fat (24.6g saturated fat); 3528kJ (844 cal); 36.2g carbohydrate; 52.4g protein; 9.8g fibre

fish in prosciutto with capers & garlic mayonnaise

6 x 360g plate-sized white fish (any firm, white-fleshed fish is suitable)
2 tablespoons finely grated lemon rind
5 cloves garlic, sliced thinly
1½ cups coarsely chopped fresh flat-leaf parsley leaves
18 slices thin prosciutto (220g)
1 tablespoon drained capers, chopped

garlic mayonnaise
½ cup (150g) mayonnaise
1 tablespoon lemon juice
1 clove garlic, crushed

1 Preheat the oven to 220°C/ 200°C fan-assisted. Line oven trays with baking parchment.
2 Wash cavity of fish under cold water; pat dry with absorbent kitchen paper.
3 Combine rind, garlic, and parsley in medium bowl; fill fish cavities with parsley mixture. Wrap three slices of the prosciutto around each fish.
4 Place fish on trays; bake 15 minutes. Sprinkle capers over fish; bake further 5 minutes or until fish is just cooked through.
5 Meanwhile, make the garlic mayonnaise.
6 Serve fish with mayonnaise and lemon wedges, if desired.

garlic mayonnaise combine ingredients in small bowl.

preparation time 15 minutes
cooking time 20 minutes
serves 6
nutritional count per serving 14.5g total fat (3.1g saturated fat); 1430kJ (342 cal); 5.7g carbohydrate; 46.3g protein; 1.6g fibre

tip for this recipe, be sure the prosciutto is very thinly sliced.

baked fish with potatoes & roasted peppers

700g salad potatoes, halved lengthways
½ cup (125ml) vegetable stock
1 tablespoon lemon juice
1 tablespoon finely grated lemon rind
⅓ cup coarsely chopped oregano
1.2kg whole white fish, cleaned
1 large red pepper (350g), sliced thinly
1 large yellow pepper (350g), sliced thinly
2 cloves garlic, crushed

1 Preheat oven to 180°C/160°C fan-assisted.
2 Combine potato, stock and juice in large baking dish; roast, uncovered, 10 minutes.
3 Meanwhile, combine rind and oregano in small bowl. Score fish both sides; press rind mixture into cuts and inside cavity.
4 Place fish in oiled large baking dish; roast, uncovered, 30 minutes.
5 Meanwhile, add peppers and garlic to potato mixture; stir to combine. Roast, uncovered, further 30 minutes until potato is tender.
6 Serve fish with vegetables, drizzled with pan juices; sprinkle with oregano leaves, if desired.

preparation time 25 minutes
cooking time 40 minutes
serves 4
nutritional count per serving 2.5g total fat (0.7g saturated fat); 1296kJ (310 cal); 28.1g carbohydrate; 40.5g protein; 5.3g fibre

tip any whole, firm, white-fleshed fish can be used for this recipe.

herb & olive fish fillets on roast potatoes

750g desiree potatoes, sliced thinly
4 cloves garlic, crushed
¾ cup coarsely chopped fresh flat-leaf parsley
¼ cup (60ml) extra virgin olive oil
4 x 200g white fish fillets
4 drained anchovy fillets, chopped finely
12 pitted black olives, halved
1 tablespoon chopped fresh basil

1 Preheat oven to 200°C/180°C fan-assisted.
2 Combine potatoes, garlic, ⅔ cup of the parsley and 2 tablespoons of the oil in medium bowl.
3 Layer potatoes in baking dish; bake, uncovered, about 50 minutes or until potato is almost tender. Place fish on potato; bake further 15 minutes.
4 Meanwhile, combine anchovies, olives, remaining parsley, basil and remaining oil in small bowl.
5 Sprinkle anchovy mixture on fish; bake further 5 minutes or until fish is just cooked through. Serve with lemon wedges, if desired.

preparation time 25 minutes
cooking time 1 hour 10 minutes
serves 4
nutritional count per serving 28.8g total fat (6.8g saturated fat); 2220kJ (531 cal); 22.3g carbohydrate; 44.3g protein; 3.6g fibre

baked potatoes

8 king edward potatoes (1.4kg), unpeeled

1 Preheat oven to 180°C/160°C fan-assisted.
2 Pierce skin of each potato with fork; wrap each potato in foil, place on oven tray. Bake 1 hour or until tender. Top with one of the variations below.

preparation time 5 minutes
cooking time 1 hour
makes 8
nutritional count per potato 0.2g total fat (0.0g saturated fat); 493kJ (118 cal); 22.9g carbohydrate; 4.2g protein; 3.5g fibre

TOPPINGS

cream cheese & pesto
combine ⅔ cup spreadable cream cheese, ½ teaspoon cracked black pepper and ⅓ cup pesto in small bowl; refrigerate until required.

preparation time 5 minutes
makes 8
nutritional count per potato 11.3g total fat (5.2g saturated fat); 966kJ (231 cal); 23.6g carbohydrate; 7.0g protein; 3.8g fibre

lime & chilli yogurt
combine ⅔ cup natural yogurt, 2 tablespoons coarsely chopped fresh coriander, 2 fresh small deseeded finely chopped red thai chillies and 1 teaspoon finely grated lime rind in small bowl; refrigerate until required.

preparation time 5 minutes
makes 8
nutritional count per potato 1.0g total fat (0.5g saturated fat); 564kJ (135 cal); 24.1g carbohydrate; 5.3g protein; 3.5g fibre

mustard & walnut butter
mash 60g softened butter, 1 teaspoon wholegrain mustard and 2 tablespoons finely chopped toasted walnuts in small bowl until mixture forms a paste; refrigerate until required.

preparation time 5 minutes
makes 8
nutritional count per potato 7.9g total fat (4.1g saturated fat); 790kJ (189 cal); 23.1g carbohydrate; 4.6g protein; 3.7g fibre

vegetables

rosemary potatoes

3kg desiree potatoes
2 tablespoons olive oil
1 tablespoon fresh rosemary leaves

1 Preheat oven to 180°C/160°C fan-assisted.
2 Make 1cm cuts in each potato, slicing about three-quarters of the way through.
3 Combine potatoes with oil in large baking dish, sprinkle with salt and freshly ground black pepper. Roast about 1 hour.
4 Increase oven temperature to 220°C/200°C fan-assisted. Roast potatoes further 15 minutes or until browned and tender. Sprinkle with rosemary.

preparation time 20 minutes
cooking time 1 hour 15 minutes
serves 10
nutritional count per serving 3.9g total fat (0.5g saturated fat); 807kJ (193 cal); 31.4g carbohydrate; 5.8g protein; 3.8g fibre

roasted butternut squash & potatoes

750g butternut squash, chopped coarsely
750g medium potatoes, chopped coarsely
1 tablespoon olive oil
2 cloves garlic, sliced thinly
2 tablespoons fresh rosemary
2 teaspoons sea salt

1 Preheat oven to 220°C/200°C fan-assisted.
2 Combine squash, potato, oil and garlic in large baking dish. Roast, uncovered, about 1 hour or until vegetables are just tender and browned lightly. Sprinkle with rosemary and salt.

preparation time 15 minutes
cooking time 1 hour
serves 4
nutritional count per serving 5.7g total fat (1.1g saturated fat); 882kJ (211 cal); 30.4g carbohydrate; 6.9g protein; 4.7g fibre

honey-glazed sweet potatoes

2.5kg sweet potatoes, unpeeled
⅔ cup (240g) honey
⅓ cup (95g) wholegrain mustard
2 tablespoons coarsely chopped fresh rosemary

1 Preheat oven to 220°C/200°C fan-assisted.
2 Halve sweet potatoes lengthways; cut each half into 2cm wedges.
3 Combine sweet potato with remaining ingredients in large bowl. Divide sweet potato mixture between two large shallow baking dishes. Roast, uncovered, about 1 hour or until sweet potato is tender and slightly caramelised.

preparation time 10 minutes
cooking time 1 hour
serves 8
nutritional count per serving 0.6g total fat (0.0g saturated fat); 1229kJ (294 cal); 62.8g carbohydrate; 5.8g protein; 5.3g fibre

roasted garlic celeriac

1 large celeriac (1.5kg)
2 tablespoons olive oil
1 medium bulb garlic (70g)
⅓ cup coarsely chopped fresh flat-leaf parsley
⅓ cup (95g) low-fat natural yogurt

1 Preheat oven to 180°C/160°C fan-assisted. Line oven tray with baking parchment.
2 Peel celeriac, cut into 3cm chunks; combine with oil in large bowl. Place celeriac and unpeeled garlic bulb on tray; roast, uncovered, turning occasionally, about 1 hour or until celeriac is tender and golden brown.
3 Cut garlic bulb in half horizontally, squeeze garlic pulp from each clove over celeriac; toss together with parsley. Serve topped with yogurt.

preparation time 15 minutes
cooking time 1 hour
serves 4
nutritional count per serving 10.1g total fat (1.4g saturated fat); 803kJ (192 cal); 11.0g carbohydrate; 7.0g protein; 15.5g fibre

hasselback potatoes

6 desiree potatoes (1.1kg), peeled, halved horizontally
40g butter, melted
2 tablespoons olive oil
¼ cup (25g) packaged breadcrumbs
½ cup (60g) finely grated cheddar cheese

1 Preheat oven to 180°C/160°C fan-assisted.
2 Place one potato half, cut-side down, on chopping board; place a chopstick on board along each side of potato. Slice potato thinly, cutting down to chopsticks to prevent cutting all the way through. Repeat with remaining potato halves.
3 Coat potato halves in combined butter and oil in medium baking dish; place, rounded-side up, in single layer. Roast, uncovered, 45 minutes, brushing frequently with oil mixture. Continue roasting without brushing about 15 minutes or until potatoes are cooked through.
4 Sprinkle combined breadcrumbs and cheese over potatoes; roast, uncovered, about 10 minutes or until topping is browned lightly.

preparation time 20 minutes
cooking time 1 hour 10 minutes
serves 4
nutritional count per serving 22.8g total fat (10.0g saturated fat); 1605kJ (384 cal); 33.0g carbohydrate; 10.0g protein; 3.8g fibre

roast potatoes

6 floury potatoes (1.3kg), peeled, halved horizontally
2 tablespoons light olive oil

1 Preheat oven to 220°C/200°C fan-assisted. Oil oven tray.
2 Boil, steam or microwave potatoes 5 minutes; drain. Pat dry with absorbent paper; cool 10 minutes.
3 Gently rake rounded sides of potatoes with tines of fork; place in single layer, cut-side down, on tray. Brush potatoes with oil.
4 Roast potatoes, uncovered, 50 minutes or until browned and crisp.

preparation time 10 minutes (plus cooling time)
cooking time 55 minutes
serves 4
nutritional count per serving 9.4g total fat (1.3g saturated fat); 1062kJ (254 cal); 34.1g carbohydrate; 6.2g protein; 4.2g fibre

tips olive oil is better than any other oil or butter as it tolerates high temperatures and lends a pleasant taste to the potatoes. Gently raking the potatoes with a fork aids crisping. Don't crowd the potatoes as they will brown unevenly; ensure the oven has reached the correct temperature before the tray goes in. King edward, desiree and maris piper potatoes are all good for roasting.

maple-glazed sweet potatoes & red onions

4 medium sweet potatoes (1.6kg)
2 tablespoons lemon juice
4 medium red onions (680g),
quartered
2 tablespoons extra virgin olive oil
2 tablespoons maple syrup
sea salt flakes

1 Preheat oven to 180°C/160°C fan-assisted. Line shallow oven tray with baking parchment.
2 Peel sweet potatoes; place in bowl of cold water with lemon juice to prevent browning. Cut sweet potatoes into thick slices, return to lemon water.
3 Drain sweet potato, pat dry with absorbent paper. Place sweet potato and onion on tray. Drizzle vegetables with oil; drizzle sweet potato only with maple syrup. Sprinkle with salt.
4 Roast vegetables about 40 minutes or until tender and browned.

preparation time 15 minutes
cooking time 40 minutes
serves 8
nutritional count per serving 4.8g total fat (0.6g saturated fat); 932kJ (223 cal); 38.6g carbohydrate; 3.6g protein; 4.5g fibre

roasted root vegetables with honey & mustard

1 tablespoon olive oil
10 baby carrots (200g), peeled, halved lengthways
2 small parsnips (120g), peeled, quartered lengthways
8 baby potatoes (320g), halved
3 baby onions (75g), halved
1 clove garlic, crushed
1 tablespoon fresh rosemary
1 tablespoon honey
2 teaspoons wholegrain mustard
1 tablespoon lemon juice

1 Preheat oven to 220°C/200°C fan-assisted.
2 Heat oil in flameproof baking dish; cook carrot, parsnip, potato and onion over heat until lightly browned, turning occasionally. Remove from heat; stir in garlic, rosemary, honey and mustard.
3 Roast vegetables, uncovered, in oven about 20 minutes or until vegetables are tender.
4 Serve vegetables drizzled with pan juices.

preparation time 10 minutes
cooking time 30 minutes
serves 2
nutritional count per serving 9.7g total fat (1.3g saturated fat); 1279kJ (306 cal); 44.3g carbohydrate; 6.3g protein; 7.8g fibre

roast beetroot & onion

2 tablespoons olive oil
10 medium unpeeled fresh beetroot (1.6kg), halved
20 baby onions (500g), peeled
2 tablespoons red wine vinegar
2 tablespoons olive oil, extra
2 tablespoons coarsely chopped flat-leaf parsley

1 Preheat oven to 240°C/220°C fan-assisted.
2 Brush base of baking dish with half of the oil, add beetroot; cover tightly with foil. Roast 45 minutes.
3 Combine onions with remaining oil, add to beetroot; cover tightly with foil. Roast 30 minutes or until tender. Remove foil; roast further 10 minutes.
4 Wearing rubber gloves, remove skin from hot beetroot; cut beetroot in half. Place beetroot and onion in serving dish; drizzle with combined vinegar and extra oil, sprinkle with parsley and freshly ground black pepper.

preparation time 25 minutes
cooking time 1 hour 25 minutes
serves 6
nutritional count per serving 12.5g total fat (1.7g saturated fat); 991kJ (237 cal); 21.9g carbohydrate; 5.5g protein; 8.0g fibre

mixed garlic mushrooms

500g flat mushrooms
⅓ cup (80ml) extra virgin olive oil
500g chestnut mushrooms
500g button mushrooms
2 cloves garlic, sliced thinly
½ cup loosely packed flat-leaf parsley leaves

1 Preheat oven to 200°C/180°C fan-assisted.
2 Place flat mushrooms in large baking dish, drizzle with half of the oil; roast, uncovered, 10 minutes.
3 Add remaining mushrooms, oil and garlic to dish; roast, uncovered, further 15 minutes or until mushrooms are tender and browned lightly. Stir in parsley.

preparation time 5 minutes
cooking time 25 minutes
serves 10
nutritional count per serving 7.8g total fat (1.0g saturated fat); 418kJ (100 cal); 0.5g carbohydrate; 5.5g protein; 4.0g fibre

garlic & herb roast tomatoes

roasted baby carrots with garlic

9 large plum tomatoes (810g), halved
1 teaspoon sea salt
1 teaspoon cracked black pepper
8 sprigs fresh thyme
2 cloves garlic, sliced thinly
¼ cup (60ml) olive oil
2 teaspoons finely chopped fresh oregano
1 teaspoon finely chopped fresh thyme

1 Preheat oven to 200°C/180°C fan-assisted.
2 Place tomatoes, cut-side up, in single layer, in large, deep baking dish. Sprinkle with combined salt, pepper, thyme sprigs, garlic and 1 tablespoon of the oil; roast, uncovered, about 1 hour or until tomato softens and browns lightly.
3 Drizzle tomato with combined chopped herbs and remaining oil.

preparation time 10 minutes
cooking time 1 hour
serves 6
nutritional count per serving 9.3g total fat (1.3g saturated fat); 426kJ (102 cal); 2.7g carbohydrate; 1.4g protein; 1.8g fibre

3 bunches baby carrots (1kg)
¼ cup (60ml) olive oil
2 cloves garlic, crushed
2 teaspoons honey
1 tablespoon fresh thyme leaves

1 Preheat oven to 220°C/200°C fan-assisted.
2 Trim carrot tops, leaving 2cm of the stems intact. Wash carrots well.
3 Place carrots in medium baking dish with combined oil, garlic and honey; toss well. Roast, uncovered, 15 minutes.
4 Add thyme leaves and roast further 3 minutes or until tender.

preparation time 15 minutes
cooking time 20 minutes
serves 10
nutritional count per serving 5.6g total fat (0.8g saturated fat); 343kJ (82 cal); 6.0g carbohydrate; 0.7g protein; 3.0g fibre

roast vegetables with harissa yogurt

1.2kg pumpkin (or butternut squash)
3 medium beetroot (500g), halved
2 medium parsnips (500g), peeled, halved lengthways
400g baby carrots, trimmed
2 medium red onions (320g), halved
2 tablespoons olive oil
50g butter, chopped
1 cup (280g) greek-style yogurt
1 tablespoon harissa

1 Preheat oven to 220°C/200°C fan-assisted.
2 Cut pumpkin into thin wedges. Place all vegetables in two large baking dishes; drizzle with oil and dot with butter.
3 Roast vegetables, uncovered, 40 minutes, turning once. Remove vegetables as they are cooked; return trays to oven further 10 minutes or until all vegetables are browned and tender.
4 Meanwhile, combine yogurt and harissa in a small bowl.
5 Serve roasted vegetables with harissa yogurt.

preparation 15 minutes
cooking time 50 minutes
serves 6
nutritional count per serving 17.2g total fat (8.0g saturated fat); 1471kJ (352 cal); 35.0g carbohydrate; 10.0g protein; 8.6g fibre

Harissa is a red chilli paste from Tunisia. Many varieties are hot, but we used quite a mild variety. It is available from gourmet food stores and delicatessens.

chipped potatoes with malt vinegar

5 medium potatoes (1kg)
1 tablespoon olive oil
2 egg whites, beaten lightly
1/3 cup (80ml) brown malt vinegar

1 Preheat oven to 220°C/200°C fan-assisted.
2 Slice potatoes thinly. Toss potato in combined oil and egg whites. Place mixture, in single layer, in oiled baking dish; sprinkle with salt and freshly ground black pepper.
3 Roast potato, uncovered, about 30 minutes or until potato is golden and crisp. Serve drizzled with malt vinegar.

preparation time 15 minutes
cooking time 30 minutes
serves 6
nutritional count per serving 3.2g total fat (0.4g saturated fat); 497kJ (119 cal); 17.5g carbohydrate; 4.0g protein; 2.1g fibre

middle-eastern roasted squash, carrot & parsnip

900g piece butternut squash (or pumpkin), unpeeled, sliced thinly
1 tablespoon olive oil
4 large carrots (720g), halved, sliced thickly
2 large parsnips (700g), chopped coarsely
⅓ cup firmly packed fresh flat-leaf parsley leaves
¼ cup (40g) roasted pine nuts

spice paste
2 cloves garlic, quartered
1 teaspoon cumin seeds
1 teaspoon coriander seeds
½ teaspoon ground cinnamon
1 teaspoon sea salt
1 tablespoon olive oil
20g butter
¼ cup (55g) firmly packed brown sugar
1½ cups (375ml) apple juice

1 Preheat oven to 200°C/180°C fan-assisted.
2 Combine pumpkin and oil in large baking dish. Roast, uncovered, about 25 minutes or until just tender.
3 Meanwhile, boil, steam or microwave carrot and parsnip, separately, until just tender; drain.
4 Make spice paste.
5 Place vegetables, parsley and nuts in large bowl with spice mixture; toss gently to combine.

spice paste using mortar and pestle or small electric spice blender, crush garlic, cumin, coriander, cinnamon, salt and oil until mixture forms a thick paste. Melt butter in large frying pan; cook paste, stirring, about 3 minutes or until fragrant. Add sugar and juice; bring to the boil. Cook, stirring, about 10 minutes or until spice mixture thickens slightly.

preparation time 20 minutes
cooking time 25 minutes
serves 8
nutritional count per serving 10.7g total fat (2.5g saturated fat); 1032kJ (247 cal); 29.9g carbohydrate; 4.8g protein; 5.8g fibre

1 medium aubergine (300g),
chopped coarsely
6 small tomatoes (540g), peeled,
chopped coarsely
4 cloves garlic, sliced thinly
1 tablespoon olive oil
2 tablespoons tomato paste
1 large red onion (300g),
chopped coarsely
1 small red pepper (150g),
chopped coarsely
1 small green pepper (150g),
chopped coarsely
2 medium courgettes (240g),
chopped coarsely
1½ cups (375ml) vegetable stock
1½ cups (300g) couscous
½ cup finely chopped fresh
flat-leaf parsley

1 Preheat oven to 200°C/180°C
fan-assisted.
2 Combine aubergine, tomato,
garlic, oil, paste, onion, pepper and
courgettes in large baking dish.
Roast, covered, 40 minutes.
Uncover; roast about 20 minutes
or until vegetables are tender.
3 Meanwhile, bring stock to the
boil in large saucepan. Stir in
couscous; cover, stand about
5 minutes or until stock is
absorbed, fluffing with fork
occasionally. Stir in parsley.
4 Serve ratatouille with couscous.

preparation time 30 minutes
cooking time 1 hour
serves 4
nutritional count per serving
6.2g total fat (0.9g saturated
fat); 1714kJ (410 cal); 71.1g
carbohydrate; 16.2g protein;
7.9g fibre

oven-roasted ratatouille with couscous

1 Preheat oven to 220°C/200°C fan-assisted.

2 Combine sweet potato, carrot, parsnip and half the combined garlic and olive oil on large shallow oven tray. Combine onion, aubergine, chilli and remaining oil mixture on separate shallow oven tray. Roast sweet potato mixture, uncovered, about 45 minutes and onion mixture, uncovered, about 30 minutes, or until vegetables are cooked and browned lightly.

3 Meanwhile, blend or process ingredients for lemon and basil dressing until smooth.

4 Just before serving, cook cheese on heated oiled grill plate until browned lightly on both sides.

5 Combine roasted vegetables with spinach; divide among serving plates. Top with cheese and drizzle with dressing.

1 medium sweet potato (400g), chopped coarsely
2 large carrots (360g), quartered lengthways
2 medium parsnips (500g), halved lengthways
2 cloves garlic, crushed
¼ cup (60ml) extra virgin olive oil
2 large red onions (600g), cut into wedges
4 baby aubergines (240g), halved lengthways

4 fresh long red chillies, halved
250g haloumi cheese, sliced
75g baby spinach leaves

lemon & basil dressing
½ cup (125ml) extra virgin olive oil
2 tablespoons lemon juice
¼ cup coarsely chopped fresh basil
1 teaspoon white sugar

preparation time 15 minutes
cooking time 45 minutes
serves 4
nutritional count per serving 53.6g total fat (12.8g saturated fat); 2880kJ (689 cal); 33.0g carbohydrate; 20.3g protein; 9.8g fibre

roasted vegetable & haloumi salad

roast potato, onion & red pepper salad

1kg new potatoes, halved
1 medium red onion (170g),
cut into thin wedges
1 large red pepper (350g),
chopped coarsely
2 teaspoons olive oil
80g baby rocket leaves
300g can red kidney beans,
rinsed, drained
100g low-fat feta, diced into
1cm pieces
2 tablespoons coarsely chopped
fresh flat-leaf parsley

honey balsamic dressing
1 tablespoon honey
2 teaspoons balsamic vinegar
2 teaspoons water
2 teaspoons olive oil

1 Preheat oven to 220°C/
200°C fan-assisted.
2 Combine potato, onion,
capsicum and oil in large deep
baking dish; roast, uncovered,
about 40 minutes or until
vegetables are browned and
tender, stirring halfway through
cooking time.

3 Place ingredients for honey
balsamic dressing in screw-top
jar; shake well.
4 Place roasted vegetables in
large bowl along with rocket,
kidney beans, feta cheese, parsley
and honey balsamic dressing; toss
gently to combine.

preparation time 15 minutes
cooking time 40 minutes
serves 4
nutritional count per serving
9.1g total fat (3.0g saturated
fat); 1501kJ (359 cal); 50.5g
carbohydrate; 17.9g protein;
9.4g fibre

glossary

allspice also called pimento or jamaican pepper; so-named as it tastes like a combination of nutmeg, cumin, clove and cinnamon. Available whole or ground.

almonds

ground also known as almond meal.

slivered small pieces cut lengthways.

artichokes

globe large flower-bud of a member of the thistle family; it has tough petal-like leaves, and is edible in part when cooked.

jerusalem neither from Jerusalem nor an artichoke, this crunchy brown-skinned tuber tastes a bit like a water chestnut and belongs to the sunflower family. Eaten raw in salads or cooked like potatoes.

aubergine also known as eggplant. Depending on their age, they may have to be sliced and salted to reduce their bitterness. Rinse and dry well before use.

barbecue sauce a spicy, tomato-based sauce used to marinate, baste or as an accompaniment.

basil An aromatic herb; there are many types, but the most commonly used is sweet basil.

bay leaves Aromatic leaves from the bay tree available fresh or dried; used to add a strong, slightly peppery flavour to soups, stocks and casseroles.

beetroot also known as beets.

breadcrumbs, stale crumbs made by grating, blending or processing 1- or 2-day-old bread.

butter we use salted butter unless stated otherwise.

buttermilk in spite of its name, it is actually low in fat. Originally the term given to the slightly sour liquid left after butter was churned from cream, today it is intentionally made from skimmed or low-fat milk to which specific bacterial cultures have been added during the manufacturing process. Available from the dairy department in supermarkets.

cajun seasoning packaged mix of herbs and spices can include paprika, basil, onion, fennel, thyme, cayenne and white pepper.

capers sold dried and salted or pickled in a vinegar brine; baby capers are also available, both in brine or dried in salt.

caraway seeds a member of the parsley family; available in seed or ground form.

cardamom native to India and used extensively in its cuisine; available in pod, seed or ground form. Has a distinctive aromatic, sweetly rich flavour and is one of the world's most expensive spices.

celeriac tuberous root with knobbly brown skin, white flesh and a celery-like flavour. Keep peeled celeriac in acidulated water to stop it from discolouring before use.

char siu sauce also known as Chinese barbecue sauce; a paste-like ingredient that is dark-red-brown in colour and possesses a sharp sweet and spicy flavour. Made with fermented soybeans, honey and spices.

cheese

haloumi Greek in origin; a crumbly textured goat's- or sheep's-milk cheese having a sharp, salty taste. Ripened and stored in salted whey.

parmesan also called parmigiano, parmesan is a hard, grainy cow's-milk cheese which originated in the Parma region of Italy. The curd for this cheese is salted in brine for a month before being aged for up to 2 years, preferably in humid conditions.

chermoulla A Moroccan blend of fresh herbs, spices and condiments, chermoulla is traditionally used for preserving or seasoning meat and fish dishes.

cherries, morello the sour variety used in jams, preserves, pies and savoury dishes, particularly as an accompaniment to game birds and meats.

chilli use rubber gloves when seeding and chopping fresh chillies as they can burn your skin. We use seeded chillies in our recipes as the seeds contain the heat; use fewer chillies rather than deseeding the lot.

flakes deep-red in colour; dehydrated, extremely fine slices and whole seeds; good for cooking or for sprinkling over cooked food.

red thai tiny and very hot.

chinese cooking wine also called shao hsing or chinese rice wine; made from fermented rice, wheat, sugar and salt with a 13.5 per cent alcohol content. Inexpensive and found in Asian food shops; if you can't find it, replace with mirin or sherry.

chives related to the onion and leek, with subtle onion flavour.

choy sum also called pakaukeo or flowering cabbage, a member of the pak choi family. Has long stems, light green leaves and yellow flowers; both stems and leaves are edible.

cinnamon available as sticks and ground into powder; one of the world's most common spices, used universally as a sweet, fragrant flavouring in both sweet and savoury dishes.

cloves dried flower buds of a tropical tree; can be used whole or in ground form. They have a strong scent and taste so should be used sparingly.

coconut

flaked dried flaked coconut flesh.

milk not the liquid inside the fruit (coconut water), but the diluted liquid from the second pressing of the white flesh of a mature coconut. Available in cans and cartons at most supermarkets.

coriander also known as cilantro, pak chee or chinese parsley; bright-green-leafed herb with a pungent aroma and taste. Coriander seeds are dried and sold whole or ground, and neither form tastes remotely like the fresh leaf.

cornflour also called cornstarch. Made from corn or wheat.

couscous a fine, grain-like cereal product made from semolina; from the countries of North Africa. It is rehydrated by steaming or with the addition of a warm liquid and swells to three or four times its original size.

crème fraîche a mature, naturally fermented cream (min. 35 per cent fat content) with a velvety texture and slightly tangy, nutty flavour. A French variation of soured cream, it can boil without curdling and is used in sweet and savoury dishes.

cumin also called zeera or comino and resembles caraway in size; is the dried seed of a plant related to the parsley family.

dill also known as dill weed; used fresh or dried, in seed form or ground; has a sweet anise/celery flavour with distinctive feathery, frond-like fresh leaves.

fennel also known as finocchio or anise; a crunchy green vegetable slightly resembling celery. Also the name given to the dried seeds of the plant which have a stronger licorice flavour.

fish sauce called naam pla (Thailand) or nuoc naam (Vietnam); the two are almost identical. Made from pulverised salted fermented fish (most often anchovies); has a pungent smell and strong taste. Available in varying degrees of intensity, so use according to your taste.

five-spice powder ingredients may vary, but is most often a mixture of ground cinnamon, cloves, star anise, sichuan pepper and fennel seeds.

flat-leaf parsley also known as continental parsley or italian parsley.

flour, plain also called all-purpose flour.

gai lan also known as gai larn, chinese broccoli and chinese kale; green vegetable appreciated more for its stems than its coarse leaves.

ginger

fresh also known as green or root ginger; the thick gnarled root of a tropical plant.

stem fresh ginger root preserved in sugar syrup; crystallised ginger can be substituted if rinsed with warm water and dried before using.

harissa a North African paste made from dried red chillies, garlic, olive oil and caraway seeds; can be used as a rub for meat, an ingredient in sauces and dressings, or eaten on its own as a condiment. It is available, ready-made, from Middle-Eastern food shops and some supermarkets.

herbs we have specified when to use fresh or dried herbs. Use dried (not ground) herbs in the proportions of 1:4 for fresh herbs, for example 1 teaspoon dried herbs instead of 4 teaspoons (1 tablespoon) chopped fresh herbs.

hoisin sauce a thick, sweet and spicy Chinese barbecue sauce made from salted fermented soybeans, onions and garlic; used as a marinade or baste, or to accent stir-fries and barbecued or roasted foods. From Asian food shops and supermarkets.

horseradish a vegetable having edible green leaves but mainly grown for its long, pungent white root. Some Asian food shops sell it fresh, but it's more common sold in bottles at the supermarket in two forms: prepared horseradish (preserved grated horseradish) and horseradish cream (a commercial creamy paste made of grated horseradish, vinegar, oil and sugar). They cannot be substituted for each other in cooking but are both used as table condiments.

juniper berries dried berries of an evergreen tree; the main flavouring ingredient in gin.

kalonji seeds also known as nigella or black onion seeds. Tiny, angular seeds, black on the outside and creamy within, with a sharp nutty flavour that can be enhanced by frying briefly in a dry hot pan before use. Are available in most Asian and Middle Eastern food shops. Often called black cumin seeds.

kecap manis Indonesian sweet, thick soy sauce which has sugar and spices added.

lemon thyme a variety of thyme with a lemony fragrance.

macadamias native to Australia, a rich and buttery nut; store in refrigerator because of its high oil content.

maple syrup distilled from the sap of maple trees found only in Canada and parts of North America. Maple-flavoured syrup or pancake syrup is not an adequate substitute for the real thing.

mushrooms

button small, cultivated white mushrooms with a mild flavour.

chestnut light to dark brown mushrooms with full-bodied flavour; suited for use in casseroles or being stuffed and baked.

enoki also known as enokitake; grown and bought in clumps, these delicately-flavoured mushrooms have small cream caps on long thin stalks. Available from Asian food shops and supermarkets.

flat a rich earthy flavour; sometimes misnamed field mushrooms.

oyster also known as abalone; grey-white mushrooms shaped like a fan. Prized for their smooth texture and subtle, oyster-like flavour.

shiitake fresh, are also called Chinese black, forest or golden oak mushrooms. Although cultivated, they have the earthiness and taste of wild mushrooms. Large and meaty, they can be used as a substitute for meat in some Asian vegetarian dishes. Dried, are called donko or dried Chinese mushrooms; have a unique meaty flavour. Rehydrate before use.

shimeji mild-flavoured, firm-textured variety resembling small oyster mushrooms but grown in clusters on banks of cottonseed hull. Colour fades as they mature, ranging from off-white to woody brown.

mustard

american mild and sweet in flavour.

dijon also called french; is a pale brown, creamy, distinctively flavoured, fairly mild French mustard.

wholegrain also called seeded. A French-style coarse-grain mustard made from crushed mustard seeds and dijon-style french mustard.

noodles, hokkien also known as stir-fry noodles; fresh wheat noodles resembling thick, yellow-brown spaghetti needing no pre-cooking before use.

oil

cooking spray we use a cholesterol-free cooking oil spray.

groundnut pressed from ground peanuts; most commonly used oil in Asian cooking because of its capacity to handle high heat without burning.

olive made from ripened olives. Extra virgin and virgin are from the first and second press, respectively, and are therefore considered the best; those labelled 'extra light' or 'light' refer to taste not fat levels.

vegetable a number of oils sourced from plant rather than animal fats.

oregano also known as wild marjoram; has a woody stalk with clumps of tiny, dark green leaves that have a pungent, peppery flavour and are used fresh or dried.

oyster sauce Asian in origin, this thick, richly flavoured brown sauce is made from oysters and their brine, cooked with salt and soy sauce, and thickened with starches.

pak choi also called bok choy or Chinese chard; has a mild mustard taste and is good braised or in stir-fries. Baby pak choi is also available.

pancetta an Italian unsmoked bacon, pork belly cured in salt and spices then rolled into a sausage shape and dried for several weeks. Used, sliced or chopped, as an ingredient rather than eaten on its own.

paprika ground dried sweet red pepper. Hot, smoked, sweet and mild are some of many grades and types available.

pattypan squash also known as baby, summer squash or scallopine. Yellow or green thin-skinned squash. pecans native to the US and now grown locally; pecans are golden brown, buttery and rich. Good in savoury as well as sweet dishes; walnuts are a good substitute.

pesto a paste made from fresh basil, oil, garlic, pine nuts and parmesan.

pine nuts also known as pignoli; not in fact a nut but a small, cream-coloured kernel from pine cones. They are best roasted before use to bring out the flavour.

pitta bread a slightly leavened, soft, flat bread. When baked, the bread puffs up, leaving a hollow, like a pocket, which can then be stuffed with savoury fillings. Pitta is also eaten with dips or soups, or toasted to form the basis of fattoush.

polenta also called cornmeal; a flour-like cereal made of dried corn (maize). Also the name of the dish made from it.

poussin a small chicken, no more than 6 weeks old, weighing a maximum of 500g.

preserved lemon a North African specialty, the citrus is preserved, usually whole, in a mixture of salt and lemon juice or oil. To use, remove and discard pulp, squeeze juice from rind, then rinse rind well before slicing thinly. Available from specialty food shops and delicatessens.

prosciutto a kind of unsmoked Italian ham; salted, air-cured and aged, it is usually eaten uncooked.

pumpkin Also known as squash; is a member of the gourd family and used as an ingredient or eaten on its own.

Various types can be substituted for one another.

quail small, delicate-flavoured game birds ranging in weight from 250g to 300g; also known as partridge.

rice, basmati a white, fragrant long-grained rice, the grains fluff up when cooked; wash several times before cooking.

risoni small rice-shape pasta; very similar to orzo.

saffron stigma of a member of the crocus family, available ground or in strands; imparts a yellow-orange colour to food once infused. The quality can vary greatly; the best is the most expensive spice in the world.

sambal oelek also ulek or olek; Indonesian in origin, this is a salty paste made from ground chillies and vinegar.

sesame seeds black and white are the most common of this small oval seed, however there are also red and brown varieties. A good source of calcium, the seeds are used in cuisines the world over as an ingredient and as a condiment. To toast, spread the seeds in a heavy-base frying pan; toast briefly over low heat.

shallots also called french shallots, golden shallots or eschalots; small, elongated, brown-skinned members of the onion family. Grows in tight clusters similar to garlic.

sichuan peppercorns also called szechuan or Chinese pepper; a mildly hot spice. Although not related to the peppercorn family, its small, red-brown aromatic berries do look like black peppercorns and have a distinctive peppery-lemon flavour and aroma.

soy sauce also called sieu; made from fermented soybeans. Several varieties are available in supermarkets and Asian food stores; we use Japanese soy sauce unless stated otherwise.

star anise a dried star-shaped pod; its seeds have an astringent aniseed flavour.

sweet potato fleshy root vegetable; available with red or white flesh.

tahini sesame seed paste available from Middle Eastern food stores; most often used in hummus and baba ghanoush.

tandoori paste Indian blend of hot and fragrant spices including turmeric, paprika, chilli powder, saffron, cardamom and garam masala.

tamarind the tamarind tree produces clusters of hairy brown pods, each of which is filled with seeds and a viscous pulp, that are dried and pressed into the blocks of tamarind found in Asian food shops. Has a sweet-sour, slightly astringent taste.

concentrate the commercial result of the distillation of tamarind juice into a condensed, compacted paste.

tomatoes

cherry also known as tiny tim or tom thumb tomatoes; small and round.

plum also called egg or roma, these are smallish, oval-shaped tomatoes much used in Italian cooking or salads.

paste triple-concentrated tomato puree used to flavour soups, stews, sauces and casseroles.

puree canned pureed tomatoes (not tomato paste). Use fresh, peeled, pureed tomatoes as a substitute, if preferred.

turmeric also called kamin; a rhizome related to galangal and ginger. Must be grated or pounded to release its acrid aroma and pungent flavour. Known for the golden colour it imparts, fresh turmeric can be substituted with the more common dried powder.

vine leaves we used vine leaves in brine (available in jars and packets).

vinegar

balsamic originally from Modena, Italy, there are now many balsamic vinegars on the market ranging in pungency and quality depending on how, and for how long, they have been aged. Quality can be determined up to a point by price; use the most expensive sparingly.

brown malt made from fermented malt and beech shavings.

cider made from fermented apples.

raspberry made from fresh raspberries steeped in a white wine vinegar.

red wine based on fermented red wine.

sherry mellow wine vinegar named for its colour.

white made from spirit of cane sugar.

white wine based on fermented white wine.

wine we use good-quality dry white and red wines in our recipes.

worcestershire sauce thin, dark-brown spicy sauce developed by the British when in India.

yogurt we use plain full-cream yogurt unless stated otherwise.

index

conversion charts

measures

The cup and spoon measurements used in this book are metric: one measuring cup holds approximately 250ml; one metric tablespoon holds 20ml; one metric teaspoon holds 5ml.

All cup and spoon measures are level. The most accurate way to measure dry ingredients is to weigh them. When measuring liquids, use a clear glass or plastic jug with metric markings.

We used large eggs with an average weight of 60g.

> **WARNING** This book may contain recipes for dishes made with raw or lightly cooked eggs. These should be avoided by vulnerable people such as pregnant and nursing mothers, invalids, the elderly, babies and young children.

dry measures

metric	imperial
15g	½oz
30g	1oz
60g	2oz
90g	3oz
125g	4oz (¼lb)
155g	5oz
185g	6oz
220g	7oz
250g	8oz (½lb)
280g	9oz
315g	10oz
345g	11oz
375g	12oz (¾lb)
410g	13oz
440g	14oz
470g	15oz
500g	16oz (1lb)
750g	24oz (1½lb)
1kg	32oz (2lb)

liquid measures

metric	imperial
30ml	1 fl oz
60ml	2 fl oz
100ml	3 fl oz
125ml	4 fl oz
150ml	5 fl oz (¼ pint/1 gill)
190ml	6 fl oz
250ml	8 fl oz
300ml	10 fl oz (½pt)
500ml	16 fl oz
600ml	20 fl oz (1 pint)
1000ml (1 litre)	1¾pints

length measures

metric	imperial
3mm	⅛in
6mm	¼in
1cm	½in
2cm	¾in
2.5cm	1in
5cm	2in
6cm	2½in
8cm	3in
10cm	4in
13cm	5in
15cm	6in
18cm	7in
20cm	8in
23cm	9in
25cm	10in
28cm	11in
30cm	12in (1ft)

oven temperatures

These oven temperatures are only a guide for conventional ovens. For fan-assisted ovens, check the manufacturer's manual.

	°C (Celcius)	°F (Fahrenheit)	gas mark
Very low	120	250	½
Low	150	275-300	1-2
Moderately low	170	325	3
Moderate	180	350-375	4-5
Moderately hot	200	400	6
Hot	220	425-450	7-8
Very hot	240	475	9

General manager Christine Whiston
Editor-in-chief Susan Tomnay
Creative director & designer Hieu Chi Nguyen
Art director Hannah Blackmore
Senior editor Wendy Bryant
Food director Pamela Clark
Sales & rights director Brian Cearnes
Marketing manager Bridget Cody
Senior business analyst Rebecca Varela
Circulation manager Jama Mclean
Operations manager David Scotto
Production manager Victoria Jefferys
International rights enquiries Laura Bamford
lbamford@acpuk.com

ACP Books are published by ACP Magazines a division of PBL Media Pty Limited
PBL Media, Chief Executive officer Ian Law
Publishing & sales director, Women's lifestyle Lynette Phillips
General manager, Editorial projects, Women's lifestyle Deborah Thomas

Editor at large, Women's lifestyle Pat Ingram
Marketing director, Women's lifestyle Matthew Dominello
Commercial manager, Women's lifestyle Seymour Cohen
Research Director, Women's lifestyle Justin Stone

Produced by ACP Books, Sydney.
Published by ACP Books, a division of ACP Magazines Ltd, 54 Park St, Sydney; GPO Box 4088, Sydney, NSW 2001.
phone (02) 9282 8618 fax (02) 9267 9438.
acpbooks@acpmagazines.com.au
www.acpbooks.com.au
Printed and bound in China.

Australia Distributed by Network Services, phone +61 2 9282 8777 fax +61 2 9264 3278 networkweb@networkservicescompany.com.au
United Kingdom Distributed by Australian Consolidated Press (UK), phone (01604) 642 200 fax (01604) 642 300 books@acpuk.com

New Zealand Distributed by Netlink Distribution Company, phone +64 9 366 9966 Fax 0800 277 412 ask@ndc.co.nz
South Africa Distributed by PSD Promotions, phone +27 11 392 6065/6/7 fax +27 11 392 6079/80 orders@psdprom.co.za
Canada Distributed by Publishers Group Canada phone (800) 663 5714; fax (800) 565 3770; service@raincoast.com

A catalogue record for this book is available from the British Library.

ISBN 978-1-903777-76-3

© ACP Magazines Ltd 2009

This publication is copyright. No part of it may be reproduced or transmitted in any form without the written permission of the publishers.